P9-BHT-443

CHOCOLATE

THE FOOD LOVER'S GUIDE
TO CHOCOLATE

Chocolate

THE FOOD LOVER'S GUIDE
TO CHOCOLATE

THUNDER BAY
P·R·E·S·S

Published in the United States by
Thunder Bay Press,
An imprint of the Advantage Publishers Group
5880 Oberlin Drive
San Diego, CA 92121-4794
www.advantagebooksonline.com

All notations of errors or omissions should be addressed to Thunder Bay Press, editorial department, at the above address. All other correspondence (author inquiries, permissions and rights) concerning the content of this book should be addressed to Quantum Books, London

QUMBCCH

ISBN 1-57145-236-2

Library of Congress Cataloging-in-Publication Data available upon request.

1 2 3 4 5 00 01 02 03 04

This book is produced by
Quantum Books
The Old Brewery, 6 Blundell Street
London N7 9BH

Designer: Bruce Low
Editor: Sarah King

This book was compiled using material from:
Divine Desserts, Chocolate Heaven, Creative Cookery: Chocolates, The Cookie book and The Baker's Bible

Manufactured in Singapore by Master Image
Printed in Singapore by Star Standard Industries Pte. Ltd.

Contents

Introduction
6
Cookies
10
Cakes and Gateaux
32
Pies and Pastries
80
Cold Desserts
96
Hot Desserts
128
Sweets and treats
144
Index
190

INTRODUCTION

The delicious and varied taste of chocolate is enjoyed all over the world, and the recipes brought together in this book include some of the most delicious sweets and desserts which are sure to satisfy even the most avid chocolate-lover.

The source of chocolate – the cocoa bean – is believed to have originated in the Amazon, where it would have grown wild. The Mayans are credited with creating the first cocoa plantations in around 600 AD, and the beans were originally used as currency, as well as forming the basis of a bitter, foamy drink, flavored with wine, and used in religious and other ceremonies.

Grown in pods, and requiring a tropical climate, the cocoa bean is grown and cultivated only in certain parts of West Africa; South America; the Caribbean and areas of Asia. Sensitive to adverse conditions and environment, cocoa trees are nurtured in special nurseries before being considered hardy enough for transporting to the plantation. It takes four or five years before the trees begin to produce a ripe crop of beans, and harvesting then takes place twice a year, with the season lasting up to three months each time. Pods are cut from the trees with machetes, then split open and the beans

and pulp removed.

The fermentation period takes up to six days, with the beans eventually drying and separating from the pulp, which is used for other by-products. To complete the drying

process, the cocoa beans are spread out to dry in the sun, and regularly checked for defects or disease. The warmth of the sun bakes the beans a dark brown color, and enhances their delicious aroma. Once completely dry, the beans are packed into sacks and sent to processing plants around the world, where they are roasted in a similar way to coffee beans, and then refined into the various types of chocolate. Although Christopher Columbus was probably the first European to see and taste the cocoa bean, it was not until the sixteenth century, during the time of the Spanish Conquistadors, that the distinctive taste became better known. At the palace of the Mexican Emperor, Montezuma, Cortez, the Spanish explorer, was introduced to the bitter chocolate drink, and immediately recognized the value of the cocoa bean as currency. Before the Spanish left Mexico, Cortez already had his own cocoa plantation, and planted more during his travels back to Spain.

Finding the Mexican chocolate drink too bitter, the Spanish sweetened it with sugar, which led to the drink becoming more and more popular. Initially a well-kept secret by the Spanish, within the next couple of centuries chocolate drinks became hugely popular and fashionable. It was introduced

to Italy in 1606, and soon spread throughout Europe.

By 1765, the first chocolate factory had been set up in America, with similar factories soon being built in Europe, particularly that owned by Dr Joseph Fry in England. A Dutchman called C Van Houten developed a process to produce cocoa powder in 1828, and in the middle of the nineteenth century Joseph Fry had combined this coca powder with sugar and chocolate liquor to produce the first eating chocolate.

Finally, in 1875, the addition of condensed milk to the mix by the Swiss Daniel Peter, introduced the first milk chocolate bar to a hungry public. Initially a treat only the rich could afford, chocolate today is one of the most common and popular foods in the world.

As technology has changed over the years, new processes have been developed so

that today there is a vast array of different types of chocolate - milk chocolate; plain, or dark chocolate; white chocolate; cooking chocolate; drinking cocoa; sweetened chocolate drinks; even low-fat chocolate. Whatever your tastes, the recipes in this book will tempt and delight you. The combination of chocolate flavors

and the mix of well-known and more unusual recipes will have chocolate-lovers everywhere reaching for their saucepans.

From easy-to-prepare sweets and treats to more complex cakes and desserts, this delicious range of recipes will be enjoyed by novices and more experienced cooks alike.

OVEN TEMPERATURES GUIDE

C	F	Gas Mark
240	475	9
230	450	8
220	425	7
200	400	6
190	375	5
180	350	4
165	325	3
150	300	2
140	275	1
125	250	1/2
110	225	1/4

Chapter One

Cookies

DELICIOUS COOKIE RECIPES,
INCLUDING SOME ATTRACTIVE
CHOCOLATE DECORATIONS

CHOCOLATE CURLS

Use chocolate at room temperature (if the chocolate is too cold the curls will break, and if it is too hot they will not curl at all). It is best to use a very thick bar of chocolate. Holding the bar over a plate, draw the blade of a vegetable peeler along the edge and allow the curls to fall on to the plate. Use a toothpick to lift the curls on to the dish to be decorated.

CHOCOLATE CUT-OUTS

Melt cooking or plain chocolate and spread evenly on greaseproof paper. Leave to set. Using cocktail cookie cutters, stamp out shapes, such as hearts, crescents, stars, animals, letters and so on.

PIPED DESIGNS

Butterflies: Cut greaseproof paper into small squares. Pipe chocolate on to the paper in a butterfly outline. Fill in the wings with additional lines. leave until beginning to set. Transfer to an unturned egg carton, placing the butterfly between the cup so it is bent in the center in the shape of a butterfly. Chill. Carefully remove the paper and position on the chosen dish.

Holly leaves: Pipe outlines and then fill the centers.

Chocolate Stem

Select non-toxic fresh leaves with clearly defined veins, such as rose, bay, ivy, strawberry or mint. Wash the leaves and pat dry. Melt some chocolate on a heatproof plate over a pan of hot water. Holding the leaf by the stem, carefully dip the veined side only into the chocolate. Alternatively, brush the chocolate on the leaf with a small paintbrush. Wipe off any chocolate that may have run onto the front of the leaf, place on greaseproof paper to set. When the chocolate is completely hard, carefully pull off the leaf by the stem.

Coconut Ice

Place the sugar and milk in a large saucepan, and heat gently, stirring until the sugar dissolves.

Bring to the boil and boil steadily to the soft ball stage, 116°C/240°F.

Remove immediately from the heat and stir in the coconut.

Add coloring if wished, and quickly pour the mixture into an oiled 8 x 6inch/20 x 15 cm shallow tin.

Leave to cool, and mark into squares or other shapes, when starting to set.

Leave to set completely, and then cut into bite-sized pieces.

Ingredients

Makes 550 g/1¼ lb

⅔ cup/450 g/1 lb granulated sugar

⅔ cup/150 ml/¼ pint milk

150 g/5 oz desccated coconut

food coloring

Chocolate Chunk Chocolate Drops

MAKES ABOUT 18

Preheat the oven to 170°C/325°F. Grease 2 large baking sheets. In a medium saucepan over low heat, melt the chocolate and butter, stirring frequently until smooth. Remove from heat to cool slightly.

With an electric mixer, beat the eggs and sugars until thick and pale, 2–3 minutes. Gradually pour in the melted chocolate, beating until well blended. Beat in the flour, cocoa powder, baking powder, vanilla extract and salt just until blended. Stir in the nuts, chocolate chips and chocolate pieces.

Drop heaping tablespoonfuls of dough on the baking sheets at least 4 inches/ 10 cm apart, flattening the dough slightly, trying to keep about 3 inch/7.5 cm circle; you will only get 4–6 cookies on each sheet. Bake for 10–12 minutes, until the tops are cracked and shiny; do not overbake or they will break when removed from the baking sheet.

Remove the baking sheets to a wire rack to cool until the cookies are firm, but not too crisp. Before they become too crisp, transfer each cookie to a wire rack to cool completely. Continue to bake in batches. Store the cookies in an airtight container.

SWEET SUCCESS

If you need to use the same baking sheets to bake in batches, cool by running the back of the baking sheet under cold water and wiping the surface with a paper towel before regreasing.

Ingredients

175 g/6 oz plain chocolate, chopped
100 g/4 oz unsalted butter, cut into pieces
2 eggs
¼ cup/100 g/4 oz sugar
¼ cup/40 g /1½ oz brown sugar
¼ cup/40 g /1½ oz flour
¼ cup/40 g/1 oz cocoa powder
1 tsp baking powder
2 tsp vanilla extract
¼ tsp salt
90 g /3½ oz pecans, toasted and chopped
175 g/6 oz plain chocolate chips
100 g/4 oz good-quality white chocolate, chopped into ¼ inch/5 mm pieces
100 g/4 oz good-quality milk chocolate, chopped into ¼ inch/5 mm pieces

INGREDIENTS

150 g /5 oz blanched whole almonds
½ cup/100 g/4 oz caster sugar
1 Tbsp cocoa powder
2 Tbsp confectioners sugar
2 egg whites
pinch of cream of tartar
1 tsp almond extract
confectioners sugar for dusting

CHOCOLATE AMARETTI COOKIES

MAKES ABOUT 24

Preheat the oven to 180°C/350°F, . Place the almonds on a small baking sheet and bake for 10–12 minutes, stirring occasionally, until golden brown. Remove from the oven and cool to room temperature; reduce the oven temperature to 170°C /325°F. Line a baking sheet with greaseproof paper or foil.

In a food processor fitted with the metal blade, process the almonds with ½ cup/50 g/2 oz sugar until the almonds are finely ground, but not oily. Transfer to a bowl and sift in the cocoa powder and confectioners sugar; stir to blend. Set aside.

With an electric mixer, beat the egg whites and cream of tartar until soft peaks form. Sprinkle in the remaining sugar, 1 tbsp at a time, beating well after each addition, until the whites are glossy and stiff. Beat in the almond extract.

Sprinkle the almond sugar mixture over and gently fold into the beaten whites just until blended. Spoon the mixture into a large piping bag fitted with a plain ½ inch/1 cm nozzle. Pipe ½ cup/1½ inch/4 cm circles about 1 inch /2.5 cm apart on to the prepared baking sheet.

Bake for 12–15 minutes, or until the biscuits appear crisp. Transfer the baking sheets to a wire rack to cool for 10 minutes. With a palette knife, transfer the biscuits to a wire rack to cool completely. When cool, dust with confectioners sugar and store in an airtight container.

VARIATION

As an alternative decoration, lightly press a few coffee-sugar crystals onto the top of each biscuit before baking.

VIENNESE CHOCOLATE COOKIES

MAKES ABOUT 20

Preheat the oven to 180°C/350°F. Cream together the butter or margarine and sugar until light and fluffy.

Work in the flour, drinking chocolate powder and cornstarch.

Put the mixture into a piping bag fitted with a large star nozzle. Pipe in fingers, or shells, or "s" shapes on to greased baking sheets.

Bake in the oven for 20–25 minutes. Cool on a wire rack.

Melt the chocolate. Dip half of each biscuit into the chocolate and leave to set on greaseproof paper.

Dust the uncoated halves of the biscuits with confectioners sugar.

VARIATION

To make chocolate gems, pipe mixture into small individual star shapes. Bake for about half the time. Place a chocolate button in the centre of each one, while still hot.

INGREDIENTS

225 g/8 oz butter or margarine

¼ cup/50 g/2 oz confectioners sugar, sieved

1⅔ cup225 g/8 oz plain flour

⅓ cup/50 g/2 oz drinking chocolate powder

¼ cup/25 g/1 oz cornstarch

100 g/4 oz plain chocolate

a little confectioners sugar

CHOCOLATE-MINT SANDWICH COOKIES

MAKES ABOUT 20

INGREDIENTS

100 g/4 oz unsalted butter, softened
¼ cup/50 g/2 oz sugar
1 egg
100 g/4 oz butter or margarine
1 tsp peppermint extract
¼ cup/25 g/1 oz cocoa powder
¾ cup/100 g/4 oz plain flour

White Chocolate Ganache Filling

½ cup/120 ml/4 floz whipping cream
175 g/6 oz good-quality white chocolate, chopped
1 tsp peppermint extract
150 g/5 oz plain chocolate, chopped
40 g/1½ oz unsalted butter

With an electric mixer, beat the butter and sugar until light and creamy, about 3 minutes. Add the egg and beat for 2–3 minutes longer, until the mixture is fluffy. Beat in the peppermint extract.

Sift the cocoa and flour together into a bowl. With a wooden spoon, gradually stir into the creamy butter mixture just until blended. Turn out the dough on to a piece of plasticwrap and use to flatten the dough to a thick disc. Wrap and refrigerate for 1 hour.

Preheat the oven to 180°C/350°F. Grease and flour 2 large baking sheets. Remove the dough from the refrigerator and divide in half. Refrigerate one half of dough.

On a lightly floured surface, roll out the other half of the dough to about ⅛ inch/3 mm thick. Using a floured heart-shaped or flower-shaped cutter, about 2 inches/5 cm in diameter, cut out as many shapes as possible and place the shapes on prepared baking sheets; reserve any trimmings. Repeat with the second half of the dough.

Bake for 7–8 minutes, until the edges are set; do not overbake as biscuits burn easily. Transfer the baking sheets to a wire rack to cool for 10 minutes. With a palette knife, transfer the biscuits to a wire rack to cool completely.

Prepare the filling. In a saucepan over medium heat, bring the cream to the boil. Remove from the heat. Add the white chocolate all at once, stirring constantly until smooth. Stir in the peppermint extract and pour into a bowl. Cool for about 1 hour until firm but not hard.

With a hand-held electric mixer, beat the white chocolate filling for 30–45 seconds, until it becomes lighter and fluffier. Spread a little white chocolate filling on to the bottom of 1 biscuit and immediately cover it with another biscuit, pressing together gently. Repeat with the remaining biscuits and filling. Refrigerate for 30 minutes, or until firm.

In a saucepan over low heat, melt the chocolate and butter, stirring frequently until smooth. Remove from the heat. Cool for 15 minutes until slightly thickened.

Spread a small amount of glaze onto the top of each sandwiched biscuit, being careful not to let the glaze drip or spread over the edges. Chill until the glaze is set.

LUXURY MACAROONS

MAKES 2 DOZEN

INGREDIENTS

150g/5 oz sweetened, flaked coconut
100g/4 oz unsalted macadamia nuts, chopped
flavorless vegetable oil for greasing
⅔ cup/160 ml/5 floz sweetened condensed milk
1 tsp vanilla extract
2 egg whites
pinch of salt
175g/6 oz white or semisweet chocolate, melted (optional)

The macadamias are a new addition and go very well with coconut.

Preheat oven to 180°C/350°F. Place flaked coconut on 1 large baking sheet and macadamia nuts on another. Toast until lightly golden, 7 to 10 minutes, stirring and shaking frequently. Pour coconut onto one plate and nuts onto another to cool completely.

Line 2 large baking sheets with non-stick baking parchment. Brush very lightly with oil. Into a large bowl, combine condensed milk, vanilla extract, flaked coconut and macadamia nuts until well-blended.

In a medium bowl with electric mixer on medium speed, beat egg whites until foamy. Add salt and increase mixer speed to high. Continue beating until whites are still but not dry. Fold whites into coconut mixture. Drop rounded tablespoonfuls onto prepared baking sheets. Bake until golden around edges, 12 to 14 minutes. Remove baking sheets to wire racks to cool completely, then gently peel off paper.

Line a large baking sheet with waxed paper. Dip macaroon bottoms into melted white or semisweet chocolate. Place on lined cookie sheet until chocolate sets, 15 to 20 minutes. Peel off paper and refrigerate in airtight containers with waxed paper between layers.

TRIPLE DECKER SQUARES

MAKES 16

Preheat the oven to 180°C/350°F. Cream together the butter or margarine and sugar until light and fluffy.

Stir in the flour. Work the dough with your hands and knead well together.

Roll out and press into a shallow 8 inch/ 20 cm square pan. Prick well with a fork.

Bake in the oven for 25–30 minutes. Cool in the pan.

To make the filling, put all the ingredients into a pan and heat gently, stirring until the sugar has dissolved. Bring to the boil and cook, stirring for 5–7 minutes until golden.

Pour the caramel over the shortbread base and leave to set.

Melt the chocolate and milk together. Spread it evenly over the caramel. Leave until quite cold before cutting into squares.

INGREDIENTS

100 g/4 oz butter or margarine

¼ cup/50 g/2 oz sugar

1¼ cup/175 g/6 oz plain flour

Filling

100 g/4 oz butter or margarine

½ cup/75 g/3 oz sugar

2 Tbsp golden syrup

¾ cup/196 g/6 oz can condensed milk

Topping

175 g/6 oz plain chocolate

2 Tbsp milk

INGREDIENTS

200 g/7 oz plain chocolate, chopped
90 g/3½ oz unsalted butter
¾ cup/150 g/5 oz caster sugar
3 eggs
1 Tbsp vanilla extract
1¼ cup/175 g/6 oz plain flour
¼ cup/25 g/1 oz cocoa powder
½ tsp baking powder
¼ tsp salt
1 cup/175–225 g/6–8 oz confectioners sugar for coating

CHOCOLATE CRACKLE TOPS

MAKES ABOUT 38

In a saucepan over low heat, melt the chocolate and butter, stirring frequently until smooth. Remove from the heat. Stir in the sugar and continue stirring for 2–3 minutes, until the sugar dissolves. Add the eggs, 1 at a time, beating well after each addition, then stir in the vanilla extract.

Into a bowl, sift together the flour, cocoa powder, baking powder and salt. Gradually stir into the chocolate mixture in batches just until blended. Cover the dough and refrigerate for 2–3 hours or overnight, until the dough is cold and holds its shape.

Preheat the oven to 170°C/325°F. Grease 2 or more large baking sheets. Place ¾ cup/150 g/5 oz confectioners sugar in a small, deep bowl. Using a small ice cream scoop, about 1 cup/1 inch/2.5 cm in diameter, or a teaspoon, scoop the cold dough into small balls.

Between the palms of your hands, roll the dough into 1½ inch/4 cm balls. Drop the balls, 1 at a time, into confectioners sugar and roll until heavily coated. Remove each ball with a slotted spoon and tap against the side of the bowl to remove excess sugar as necessary; you may need to cook in batches.

Bake the biscuits for 10–12 minutes, or until top of biscuit feels slightly firm when touched with fingertip; do not overbake or biscuits will be dry. Transfer the baking sheets to a wire rack for 2–3 minutes, just until the biscuits are set. With a palette knife, transfer the biscuits to a wire rack to cool completely.

SWEET SUCCESS

These biscuits are best eaten as fresh as possible, but they will last for several days in an airtight container.

TRUFFLES

MAKES 12

Melt the chocolate in the top of a double boiler.

Pour the chocolate into a mixing bowl with the cream, ground almonds, rum or brandy and crumbs.

Mix well and chill for 1 hour, or until it is firm enough to handle.

Divide the chocolate mixture into 12 pieces. Roll into small balls and toss in sifted sugar or chocolate strands.

VARIATION

Melt the chocolate as before.

Mix with the softened butter, yolks and cream.

Chill and shape truffles as above. Roll in sugar or chocolate strands.

INGREDIENTS

100 g/4 oz plain (dark) chocolate in small pieces
3 Tbsp light cream
100 g/4 oz ground almonds
2 Tbsp rum or brandy
225 g/8 oz cookie or cake crumbs
½ cup/100 g/4 oz confectioners sugar or
50 g/2 oz chocolate strands

Variation

225 g/8 oz plain chocolate in small pieces
2 Tbsp/30 g butter
2 egg yolks
2 tsp light cream
½ cup/100 g/4 oz confectioners sugar or
50 g/2 oz chocolate strands

FLORENTINES

MAKES 40

Preheat the oven to 180°C/350°F.

Place the butter, sugar and cream in a heavy-bottomed pan. Heat over a low flame, stirring constantly, until the sugar has dissolved.

Remove the butter from the heat and stir in the chopped nuts and fruit.

Grease flat baking trays and line with rice paper or edible parchment.

Drop small spoonfuls of the cookie mixture onto the baking trays. Be sure to leave as much space as possible between them as they spread while they are baking.

Bake for 10 minutes and leave to cool on the trays for at least 5 minutes.

Move to a cooling rack and trim extra paper.

To make the icing, sift together the sugar and cocoa.

Combine half of the sugar with the butter and beat well.

Gradually add the remaining sugar, alternating with the combined milk and vanilla.

When the Florentines have cooled completely, turn them upside down and spread with the confectioners. Leave to set before serving.

INGREDIENTS

100 g/4 oz butter
½ cup/100 g/4 oz sugar
1 tbsp heavy cream
100 g/4 oz almonds, chopped
50 g/2 oz candied cherries
50 g/2 oz white raisins

Confectioners

1⅛ cup/225 g/8 oz confectioners sugar
6 tbsp/90 g unsweetened cocoa
50 g/2 oz butter
6 Tbsp milk
1 tsp vanilla extract

CHOCOLATE CRISPIES

MAKES 24

INGREDIENTS

175 g/6 oz butter
175 g/6 oz chocolate
¾ cup/175 ml/6 floz golden (light corn) syrup
175 g/6 oz cornflakes or rice crispies

Melt the butter, chocolate and syrup together in the top of a double boiler. Mix well.

Pour the sauce over the cornflakes or rice crispies and stir well,

Place 24 paper cups (as for muffins or cupcakes) in a pan and spoon the cereal mixture into the cases.

Leave to set for at least 8 hours.

VARIATION
Press the cereal mixture into the paper cups leaving a hollow space in the center which can later be filled with fruit and/or cream.

Chapter Two

Cakes and Gateaux

RICH AND TASTY TREATS, FEATURING RECIPES FROM AROUND THE WORLD

White Chocolate and Coconut Layer Cake

SERVES 12–16

Preheat the oven to 180°C/350°F. Grease and flour 9 inch/23 cm round, 2 inch/ 5 cm deep cake tins.

In the top of a double boiler over a low heat, melt the chocolate with the cream, stirring until smooth. Stir in the milk and rum; set aside to cool.

With an electric mixer, beat the butter with the sugar until pale and thick, about 5 minutes. Add the eggs, 1 at a time, beating well after each addition. In another bowl, stir together the flour, baking powder and salt. Alternately add the flour mixture and melted white chocolate in batches, just until blended; stir in half the coconut. Pour the batter into the tins and spread evenly.

Bake for 20–25 minutes, until a fine skewer inserted in the centers comes out clean. Cool on a wire rack for 10 minutes. Unmold the cakes on to the wire rack and cool completely.

Meanwhile, prepare the mousse. In a saucepan over a low heat, melt the white chocolate and 1½ cups/350 ml/12 floz cream, stirring frequently until smooth. Stir in the rum, then pour into a bowl. Refrigerate for 1–1½ hours, until completely cold and thickened.

Whip the remaining cream until soft peaks form. Stir 1 spoonful of cream into the mousse mixture to lighten, then fold in about 1 cup/250 ml/8 floz whipped cream.

With a serrated knife, slice the cake layers in half horizontally, making 4 layers. Place 1 layer on a plate and spread one-sixth of the mousse on top. Sprinkle with one-third of the remaining coconut. Place a second layer on top and spread with one-sixth of mousse. Sprinkle with another third of coconut. Place a third layer on top and spread with another one-sixth of mousse and the remaining coconut. Cover with the last cake layer and cover the top and sides with the remaining mousse.

Spread the remaining whipped cream over the top and sides of the cake and garnish with fresh coconut strips.

Ingredients

100g/4 oz good-quality white chocolate, chopped
½ cup/120 ml/4 floz whipping cream
½ cup/120 ml/4 floz milk
1 Tbsp light rum
100 g/4 oz unsalted butter, softened
1 cup/175 g/6 oz sugar
3 eggs
1⅔ cup/225 g/8 oz plain flour
1 tsp baking powder
pinch of salt
75 g/3 oz shredded sweetened coconut

White Chocolate Mousse

425 g/15 oz good-quality white chocolate, chopped
4 cups/1 litre/1¼ pt whipping cream
½ cup/120 ml/4 floz light rum
fresh coconut strips for decoration

DOBOS TORTE

SERVES 8

INGREDIENTS

6 eggs, separated
zest of 1 lemon, grated
1 cup/175 g/6 oz sugar
1 cup/150 g/5 oz plain flour, sieved

Butter cream

225 g/8 oz plain chocolate
225 g/8 oz butter
2½ cup/450 g/1 lb confectioners sugar sieved

Caramel

1 cup/175 g/6 oz granulated sugar

Preheat the oven to 200°C/400°F. Grease and flour 7 flat surfaces, such as baking sheets and roasting tins. Using a cake tin or plate, mark a circle 8 inch/20 cm in diameter on each one.

Whisk the egg yolks with the lemon zest and sugar in a mixing bowl until the mixture is thick.

Whisk the egg whites until stiff.

Fold the egg whites and flour alternately into the egg yolk mixture.

Divide the mixture evenly between the circles. bake in batches in the oven for about 8 minutes, or until golden brown. Lift on to wire racks to cool.

Use the 8 inch/20 cm cake tin or plate to trim the edges so that all the circles are the same size.

To make the butter cream, melt the chocolate. Add the butter and stir until melted. Cool. Beat in the sieved confectioners sugar.

To make the caramel, put the sugar into a heavy saucepan. Heat very slowly over a low heat, stirring until the sugar is completely dissolved. Heat until the caramel turns golden brown.

Pour the caramel immediately onto one of the cake layers. Before the caramel sets, cut the cake layer into 8 sections, using an oiled or buttered knife.

Sandwich the remaining cake layers together with some of the chocolate butter cream. Spread butter cream round the sides of the cake.

Put the remaining butter cream into a piping bag, fitted with a star nozzle. Pipe eight long whirls on top of the cake, radiating out from the center. Set a caramel-coated section, tilted slightly, on each whirl.

Chocolate Butter Biscuits

MAKES ABOUT 36

Ingredients

175 g/6oz flour
60 g/2oz unsweetened cocoa powder
1/4 tsp salt
175 g/6oz sugar
1 egg yolk
1 tsp almond or vanilla essence
50 g/2 oz plain chocolate
60 g/2 oz unblanched chopped almonds, toasted

Pre-heat the oven to 375°F/190°C/Gas 5. In a medium bowl, sift together the flour, cocoa powder and salt.

In a large bowl, with an electric mixer, beat the butter until creamy, 30 seconds. Gradually add the sugar and beat until light and fluffy. 1 to 2 minutes. Add the egg yolk and almond or vanilla essence, and beat for 1 minute. Gradually stir in the flour mixture until well-blended.

Using a teaspoon to scoop the dough and also using your palms, form into 5-cm/2-inch logs. Place logs 2.5cm/1inch apart on greased baking sheets on wire racks to cool completely.

Arrange the logs on a wire rack placed over a baking sheet to catch any drips. Using a teaspoon or paper cone, drizzle with chocolate in a zigzag pattern, then sprinkle over a few chopped almonds. Leave to set. Store in airtight containers.

Tip

Cookies can be shaped into 1 1/2 inch balls, decorated with half a candied cherry, or dusted with sugar.

Saucy Chocolate Cake

SERVES 8

Preheat the oven to 180°C/350°F. Lightly butter a 8 x 8 x 2 inch/20 x 20 x 5 cm baking dish.

Combine the flour, sugar, 3 tbsp of cocoa powder, baking powder and salt. Stir in the milk, butter and vanilla extract just until blended. Spoon into the dish and spread evenly.

In another bowl, combine the brown sugar, chopped nuts and remaining cocoa; gradually stir in the boiling water until the sugar dissolves. Gently pour over the batter in the baking dish.

Bake for 25–30 minutes, until the top of the cake springs back when touched with a fingertip. Cool for 30–40 minutes on a wire rack. Dust with confectioners sugar and serve warm or chilled.

Ingredients

¾ cup/100 g/4 oz plain flour
½ cup/90 g/3½ oz sugar
5 Tbsp cocoa powder
2 tsp baking powder
½ tsp salt
¾ cup/175 ml/6 floz milk
25 g/1 oz butter
1 tsp vanilla extract

Topping

¾ cup/150 g/5 oz light brown sugar
50 g/2 oz chopped pecans (optional)
1⅔ cups/400 ml/14 floz boiling water
confectioners sugar for dusting

CLASSIC BROWNIES

MAKES ABOUT 20

INGREDIENTS

1¼ cups/225 g/8 oz soft brown sugar
⅓ cup/50 g/2 oz unsweetened cocoa powder, sieved
½ cup/75 g/3 oz self-rising flour
2 eggs
2 Tbsp milk
100 g/4 oz butter, melted
50 g/2 oz walnuts, finely chopped
50 g/2 oz raisins, chopped
walnut halves, to decorate

Confectioners

100 g/4 oz plain chocolate
1 Tbsp black coffee

Preheat the oven to 180°C/350°F. Mix together the sugar, cocoa and flour.

Beat together the eggs and milk. Stir into the flour mixture, together with the butter, walnuts and raisins.

Spread in a greased and base-lined pan measuring 7 x 11 x 1½ inches/18 x 28 x 4 cm.

Bake in the oven for about 30 minutes. Cool.

Melt the chocolate and coffee together. Spread over the cake.

To serve, decorate with walnut halves. Cut into squares when cold.

Sachertorte

SERVES 8

Ingredients

225 g/8 oz plain chocolate
100 g/4 oz unsalted butter
1 cup/175 g/6 oz caster sugar
5 eggs, separated
75 g/3 oz ground hazelnuts or almonds
⅓ cup/50 g/2 oz self-rising flour, sieved

Filling

⅔ cup/150 ml/¼ pt heavy cream, whipped

Confectioners

225 g/8 oz plain chocolate
100 g/4 oz butter, melted

To decorate

whipped cream
whole hazelnuts
chocolate leaves (see page 12/13)

Preheat the oven to 180°C/350°F. Melt the chocolate in a bowl over a saucepan of hot water. Add the butter, cut into small pieces, and beat until the butter has melted and the mixture is smooth.

Beat in the caster sugar. Gradually add the egg yolks, beating well between each addition.

Whisk the egg whites until stiff. Gently fold into the chocolate, with the ground nuts and flour.

Put the mixture into two greased and base-lined 8 inch/20 cm sandwich cake tins. Bake for 20–25 minutes. Cool on a wire rack.

When the cakes are cold, sandwich together with whipped cream.

To make the icing, melt the chocolate and gradually add the butter, beating well between each addition. Leave for 20–30 minutes, until cold, and of a coating consistency.

Spread the icing over the top and sides of the cake. Leave until set.

Decorate with piped whipped cream, hazelnuts and chocolate leaves.

Chunky Chocolate Brownies with Fudge Glaze

MAKES 14–16

Preheat the oven to 180°C/350°F. Invert a 8 inch/20 cm square baking tin and mold a piece of foil over the bottom. Turn the tin over and line with the molded foil. Lightly grease foil.

In a saucepan over low heat, melt the chocolate and butter, stirring frequently until smooth. Remove the pan from the heat.

Stir in the sugars and continue stirring for 2 minutes longer, until the sugar is dissolved. Beat in the eggs and vanilla extract. Stir in the flour until blended. Stir in the nuts and chopped chocolate. Pour into the lined tin.

Bake for 20–25 minutes, until a cocktail stick or fine skewer inserted 2 inches/5 cm from the centre comes out with just a few crumbs attached; do not overbake. Transfer to a wire rack to cool for 30 minutes. Using the foil as a guide, remove the brownie from the tin and cool on the rack for at least 2 hours.

Prepare the glaze. In a saucepan over medium heat, melt the chocolate, butter, golden syrup, vanilla extract and coffee powder, stirring frequently until smooth. Remove from the heat. Refrigerate for 1 hour, or until thickened and spreadable.

Invert the brownie onto a plate and remove the foil. Invert back on to the rack and slide on to a serving plate, top-side up. Using a palette knife, spread a thick layer of glaze over the top of the brownie just to the edges. Refrigerate for 1 hour, until set. Cut into squares or bars.

Ingredients

275 g/10 oz bittersweet chocolate, chopped
50 g/2 oz unsalted butter cut into pieces
3/8 cup/75 g/3 oz brown sugar
50 g/2 oz granulated sugar
2 eggs
1 Tbsp vanilla extract
50 g/2 oz plain flour
90 g/3 1/2 oz pecans or walnuts, chopped and toasted
150 g/5 oz good-quality white chocolate, chopped into 5 mm pieces

Fudgy chocolate glaze

175 g/6 oz plain chocolate, chopped
50 g/2 oz unsalted butter, cut into pieces
2 Tbsp golden syrup
2 tsp vanilla extract
1 tsp instant coffee powder

SURPRISE CHOCOLATE RING

SERVES 8

Preheat the oven to 180°C/350°F. Sieve the flour and cocoa into a mixing bowl. Add the margarine, sugar and eggs. Beat well together.

Spoon the mixture into a greased and floured 5 cups/1.2 litre/2 pt ring mold. Bake in the oven for about 35–40 minutes. Turn out and cool.

Turn the cake upside down and cut a slice about ¾ inch/2 cm deep off the flat base of the ring. Lift off the slice carefully and reserve.

With a teaspoon, scoop out the cake in a channel about ¾ inch/2 cm deep and 1 inch/2.5 cm wide.

Sprinkle 3 tbsp of the cherry brandy over the sponge.

Chop the fruit and spread in the hollow.

Whisk the cream until stiff. Stir in the remaining brandy. Spread the cream over the fruit.

Place the reserved slice back on the cake.

Invert the cake so it is the right way up.

To make the confectioners, put the cream into a saucepan and bring just to the boil. Add the chocolate. Stir until the chocolate melts.

Cool until the mixture is thick and smooth. Pour over the cake.

Put in a cool place until set.

Decorate with piped chocolate butterflies or chocolate dipped fruit.

INGREDIENTS

1 cup/150 g/5 oz self-rising flour
¼ cup/25 g/1 oz unsweetened cocoa powder
175 g/6 oz soft margarine
1 cup/175 g/6 oz sugar
3 eggs
60 ml/4 Tbsp cherry brandy
100 g/4 oz fruit (eg strawberries, raspberries, stoned cherries)
⅔ cup/150 ml/¼ pt heavy cream

Confectioners

¼ cup/65 ml/2½ floz double cream
175 g/6 oz plain chocolate, grated

To decorate

Piped chocolate butterflies (see page 12/13) or chocolate dipped fruits

COCOA BROWNIE WITH MILK CHOCOLATE AND WALNUT TOPPING

SERVES 12

INGREDIENTS

⅓ cup/50 g/2 oz plain flour
¼ cup/40 g/1½ oz cocoa powder
¼ tsp baking powder
¼ tsp salt
100 g/4 oz unsalted butter
1¼ cup/225 g/8 oz sugar
2 eggs
2 tsp vanilla extract
75 g/3 oz walnuts, coarsely chopped

Milk chocolate and walnut topping

175–200 g/6–7 oz milk chocolate
75 g/3 oz walnuts, chopped

Preheat the oven to 180°C/350°F. Grease a 9 inch/23 cm springform tin or 9 inch/23 cm cake tin with a removable bottom. Into a bowl sift the flour, cocoa powder, baking powder and salt. Set aside.

In a medium saucepan over medium heat, melt the butter. Stir in the sugar and remove from the heat, stirring 2–3 minutes to dissolve the sugar. Beat in the eggs and vanilla extract. Stir in the flour mixture just until blended; then stir in the walnuts. Pour into the prepared tin, smoothing the top evenly.

Bake for 18–24 minutes, until a toothpick or fine skewer inserted 2 inches /5 cm from the center comes out with just a few crumbs attached; do not overbake or the brownie will be dry.

Prepare the topping. Break the milk chocolate into pieces. As soon as the brownie tests done, remove from the oven to a heatproof surface. Quickly place the chocolate pieces all over the top of the brownie; do not let the chocolate touch the side of the tin. Return to the oven for 20–30 seconds.

Remove the brownie and, with the back of a spoon, gently spread the softened chocolate evenly over the top. Sprinkle walnuts evenly over the top and, with the back of a spoon, gently press them into the chocolate. Cool on a wire rack for 30 minutes.

Refrigerate for 1 hour, until set. Run a knife around the edge of the tin to loosen the brownie from the edge. Carefully remove the side of the tin. Cool completely and serve at room temperature.

MUSHROOM CAKE

SERVES 6

INGREDIENTS

¼ cup/25 g/1 oz unsweetened cocoa powder
1 Tbsp boiling water
½ cup/100 g/4 oz butter or margarine
100 g/4 oz light, soft brown sugar
2 eggs, beaten
¾ cup/100 g/4 oz self-raising flour

Icing

100 g/4 oz butter or margarine
1¼ cup/225 g/8 oz confectioners sugar
50 g/2 oz plain chocolate, melted
225 g/8 oz marzipan (preferably "white")
apricot jelly, sieved
confectioners sugar or drinking chocolate

Preheat the oven to 180°C/350°F. Mix together the cocoa powder and water to form a paste.

Put the butter or margarine, sugar and chocolate paste into a bowl and beat until light and fluffy.

Beat in the eggs a little at a time.

Fold in the flour.

Spread the mixture into 1 greased and base-lined, 8 inch/20 cm sandwich cake tin. Bake in the oven for about 25 minutes. Turn out and cool.

To make the icing, cream together the butter or margarine and confectioners sugar. Stir in the melted chocolate and beat well. Cool.

Using a piping bag fitted with a star nozzle, pipe lines of icing from the edge of the cake to the center, to represent the underside of a mushroom.

Reserve a small piece of marzipan for the stalk. Roll the remaining marzipan out to a strip about 24 inch/60 cm long and wide enough to stand just above the sides of the cake.

Brush the sides of the cake with apricot jelly. Press the marzipan strip round the edge of the cake. Curve the top of the marzipan over the piped ridges.

Shape the reserved marzipan into a stalk and place in the center of the cake. Sieve a little confectioners sugar or drinking chocolate over the confectioners on the cake.

Triple Chocolate Cheesecake

SERVES 18–20

Preheat the oven to 180°C/350°F. Lightly grease the bottom and sides of a 10 inch/25 cm, 3 inch/7.5 cm deep springform tin.

Prepare the crust. In a food processor, process the chocolate biscuits until fine crumbs form. Pour in the melted butter and cinnamon. Process until just blended. Pat onto the bottom and to within ½ inch/1 cm of the top of the sides of the tin.

Bake for 5–7 minutes, just until set. Remove to a wire rack to cool while you prepare the filling. Lower the oven temperature to 170°C/325°F.

Prepare the filling. In a saucepan over low heat, melt the chocolate and butter, stirring frequently until smooth. Set aside to cool; stir in the soured cream.

With an electric mixer, beat the cream cheese and sugar until smooth, 2–4 minutes. Add the eggs, 1 at a time, beating well after each addition, scraping the bowl occasionally. Slowly beat in the chocolate mixture and vanilla extract just until blended. Pour into the baked crust. Place the tin on a baking sheet; place a small saucepan of water on the floor of the oven to create moisture.

Bake for 1–1½ hours, or until the edge of the cheesecake is set but the center is still slightly soft. Turn off the oven but leave the cheesecake in the oven for another 30 minutes. Remove to a wire rack to cool. Run a knife around the edge of the cheesecake in the tin to separate it from the side; this helps to prevent cracking. Cool to room temperature.

Prepare the glaze. In a saucepan, melt the chocolate with the cream and vanilla extract, stirring until smooth. Cool and leave to thicken slightly, 10–15 minutes. Pour over the warm cake in the tin; cool the glazed cake completely. Using strips of greaseproof paper dust cocoa in horizontal bands across the top of the cake. Refrigerate, loosely covered, overnight.

To serve, run a knife around the edge of the tin to loosen the cheesecake. Remove the side of the tin. If you like, slide a knife under the crust to separate the cheesecake from the base, and, with a palette knife, slide it on to a serving plate.

Ingredients

225 g/8 oz plain chocolate digestive biscuits
50 g/2 oz butter, melted
½ tsp ground cinnamon

Filling

450 g/1 lb plain chocolate, chopped
50 g/2 oz butter, cut into pieces
1 cup/250 ml/8 floz soured cream
900 g/2 lb cream cheese, softened
1¼ cups/225 g/8 oz sugar
5 eggs
1 tbsp vanilla extract

Chocolate glaze

100 g/4 oz plain chocolate, chopped
½ cup/120 ml/4 floz heavy cream
1 tsp vanilla extract
cocoa powder

FAMILY CHOCOLATE CAKE

SERVES 8–10

Preheat the oven to 180°C/350°F. Put the chocolate and honey into a small bowl over a pan of hot water. Stir until the chocolate has melted. Cool.

Cream together the butter or margarine and sugar until light and fluffy.

Beat in the chocolate mixture, then the eggs.

Sieve together the flour, cocoa powder and baking powder.

Stir in the flour mixture a little at a time, alternately with the vanilla extract and milk.

Pour the mixture into a lined 7½ inch/19 cm round cake tin.

Bake in the oven for about 45 minutes.

Turn on to a wire rack, leaving the lining paper on the cake to form a collar.

When the cake is cool, make the icing. Put the chocolate and water into a small saucepan and melt over a gentle heat.

Remove from the heat and stir in the butter. When the butter has melted, beat in the confectioners sugar.

Spread the icing over the top of the cake and swirl with a palette knife. When the icing is firm, remove the lining paper from the cake.

INGREDIENTS

75 g/3 oz plain chocolate
50 g/2 oz clear honey
100 g/4 oz butter or margarine
⅜ cup/75 g/3 oz sugar
2 eggs
1 cup/150 g/5 oz self-rising flour
¼ cup/25 g/1 oz unsweetened cocoa powder
1½ level tsp baking powder
¼ tsp vanilla extract
⅔ cup/150 ml/¼ pt milk

Icing

50 g/2 oz plain chocolate
3 Tbsp water
25 g/1 oz butter
1 cup/200 g/7 oz confectioners sugar, sieved

Chocolate Boxes

MAKES 9

Ingredients

1 egg
⅛ cup/25 g/1 oz sugar
¼ cup/25 g/1 oz plain flour

Filling

⅔ cup/150 ml/¼ pt water
150 g/5 oz pkt tangerine jelly
225 g/8 oz curd cheese
1¼ cup/300 ml/½ pt heavy cream
2 Tbsp apricot jelly, sieved

To decorate

2 inch/36 x 5 cm chocolate squares (see page 12/13)
whipped cream
9 mandarin orange segments
quartered walnuts

Preheat the oven to 200°C/400°F. Whisk the egg and sugar together until the mixture is thick and creamy and the whisk leaves a trail when lifted.

Using a metal spoon, gently fold in the flour. Pour into a shallow greased and base-lined 7 inch/18 cm square tin.

Bake for 10–12 minutes. Turn out and cool.

Heat the water. Add the jelly and stir until dissolved. Chill until the mixture begins to turn syrupy.

Beat the cheese and gradually add the jelly.

Whip the cream until thick and fold into the cheese mixture. Pour into an 7 inch/18 cm square cake tin, lined with greaseproof paper. Chill until set.

Spread the sponge with apricot jelly. Unmold the cheese mixture on to the sponge. Trim the edges.

Cut the cake into nine squares. Press a chocolate square on to each side of each cake.

To serve, pipe whipped cream on top of each chocolate box. Top with mandarins and walnuts.

VARIATIONS

Use cherry Jelly, cherry jelly and top with canned or fresh cherries.

Use strawberry/raspberry jelly, and top with fresh strawberries/raspberries.

Use lemon jelly, lemon curd and top with pieces of canned or fresh pineapple.

Use lime jelly, lime marmalade and top with halved slices of kiwi fruit.

Chocolate Pecan Torte

SERVES 16

Ingredients

200 g/7 oz plain chocolate, chopped
150 g/5 oz pieces unsalted butter
4 eggs
½ cup/100 g/4 oz sugar
2 tsp vanilla extract
90 g/3½ oz ground pecans
24 pecan halves

Chocolate honeyglaze

100 g/4 oz plain chocolate, chopped
50 g/2 oz pieces unsalted butter
2 Tbsp honey

Preheat the oven to 180°C/350°F. Grease a 8 inch/20 cm, 2 inch/5 cm deep springform tin; line the bottom with greaseproof paper and grease the paper. Wrap the bottom of the tin in foil.

In a saucepan over a low heat, melt the chocolate and butter, stirring until smooth. Remove from the heat.

With an electric mixer, beat the eggs with sugar and vanilla extract just until frothy, 1–2 minutes. Stir in the melted chocolate and ground nuts until well blended. Pour into the tin and tap gently on a work surface to break any large air bubbles.

Place the tin into a larger roasting tin and pour boiling water into the roasting tin, about ¾ inch/2 cm up the side of the springform tin. Bake for 25–30 minutes, until the edge of the cake is set, but the center is still soft. Remove the tin from the waterbath and remove the foil. Cool on a wire rack completely.

Meanwhile, place the pecan halves on a baking sheet and bake for 10–12 minutes, until just brown, stirring occasionally.

In a saucepan over a low heat, melt the chocolate, butter and honey, stirring until smooth; remove from the heat. Carefully dip the roasted nuts halfway into the glaze and place on a greaseproof paper-lined baking sheet until set. The glaze will have thickened slightly.

Remove the side of the tin and turn the cake on to a wire rack placed over a baking sheet to catch any drips. Remove the tin bottom and paper so the bottom of cake is now the top. Pour the thickened glaze over the cake, tilting the rack slightly to spread the glaze. If necessary, use a palette knife to smooth the sides. Arrange the nuts around the outside edge of the torte and leave the glaze to set. With a palette knife, carefully slide the cake on to a serving dish.

SWEET SUCCESS

This cake can be baked 2–3 days ahead, wrapped tightly and refrigerated or even frozen. Bring to room temperature before glazing.

Cream Cheese-Marbled Brownies

SERVES 15–20

Ingredients

250 g/9 oz bittersweet chocolate, chopped
225 g/8 oz unsalted butter, softened
1¼ cup/225 g/8 oz granulated sugar
¼ cup/50 g/2 oz soft brown sugar
3 eggs
1 tbsp vanilla extract
¾ cup/100 g/4 oz plain flour
¼ tsp salt
450 g/1 lb cream cheese, softened
1 egg
1 tsp vanilla extract
finely grated zest of 1 lemon

Preheat the oven to 180°C/350°F. Invert a 9 x 13 inch/23 x 32.5 cm baking tin and mold foil over the bottom. Turn the tin over and line with the foil; leave the foil to extend above the sides of the tin. Grease the bottom and sides of the foil.

In a saucepan over low heat, melt the chocolate and 4 oz/100 g of the butter, stirring frequently until smooth. Remove from the heat. Cool to room temperature.

In a bowl, using a hand-held mixer, beat the remaining butter, 5 oz/150 g granulated sugar and the brown sugar until light and creamy, 2–3 minutes. Add the eggs, 1 at a time, beating well after each addition. Beat in the vanilla extract, then slowly beat in the melted chocolate and butter. Stir in the flour and salt just until blended.

In a bowl, using a hand-held electric mixer, beat the cream cheese and remaining sugar until smooth, about 1 minute. Beat in the egg, vanilla extract and lemon zest.

Pour two-thirds of the brownie batter into the tin and spread evenly. Pour the cream cheese mixture over the brownie layer. Spoon the remaining brownie mixture in dollops on top of the cream cheese mixture in 2 rows along the long side of the tin. Using a knife or spoon, swirl the brownie batter into the cream cheese batter to create a marbled effect.

Bake for 25–35 minutes, or until a toothpick or fine skewer inserted 2 inches/5 cm from the edge of the tin comes out with just a few crumbs attached. Transfer to a wire rack to cool in the tin.

When cool, use the foil to help lift the brownie out of the tin. Invert on to another rack or baking sheet and peel off the foil. Invert back on to the wire rack and slide on to a serving plate. Cut into squares and wrap and refrigerate; or wrap until ready to serve, then cut into squares.

INGREDIENTS

50 g/2 oz butter or margarine, cut in pieces
⅔ cup/150 ml/¼ pt water
½ cup/65 g/2½ oz plain flour
2 eggs, beaten

Filling

⅔ cup/150 ml/¼ pt heavy cream
225 g/8 oz fresh raspberries
a little sugar

Topping

175 g/6 oz plain chocolate
25 g/1 oz butter

RASPBERRY CHOCOLATE ECLAIRS

MAKES ABOUT 10

Preheat the oven to 200°C/400°F. Put the butter or margarine and water into a pan and bring to the boil.

Remove from the heat and tip all the flour into the pan at once. Beat with a wooden spoon until the paste forms a ball. Cool.

Whisk the eggs into the paste, a little at a time. Continue beating until the mixture is glossy.

Put the pastry into a piping bag fitted with a large plain nozzle. Pipe 3 inch/7.5 cm lengths on to greased baking sheets.

Bake in the oven for about 25 minutes, until golden brown.

Remove from the oven and make a couple of slits in the sides of each one to allow steam to escape. Return to the oven for a few minutes to dry. Cool on a wire rack.

To make the filling, whisk the cream until stiff. Fold in the raspberries and sugar to taste.

Make a slit down the side of each eclair and fill with the cream mixture.

Melt together the chocolate and butter. Dip the tops of the eclairs into the chocolate and then leave to set.

Red Velvet Cake

SERVES 10–12

Preheat the oven to 180°C/350°F. Cream the margarine and sugar until fluffy.

Beat in the eggs.

Make a paste of the food coloring and cocoa. Add to the butter mixture and blend well.

Sift the flour and salt. Gradually add to the butter mixture, alternating with the buttermilk and vanilla.

Stir the bicarbonate of soda into the vinegar in a large spoon, holding it over the mixing bowl as it foams. Add to the cake mixture stirring well.

Grease two 8 inch/20 cm cake pans. Divide the mixture between the two pans and bake for 30 minutes. Cool.

To prepare the icing, stir the flour, sugar and milk over a very low heat until thick.

Cream the butter with the vanilla until it is very light.

Beat the cooked mixture into the butter until the icing has the texture of whipped cream.

To assemble the cake, place one layer, upside down, on a serving dish. Spread with one third of the icing. Gently place the second layer, right side up, on top. Spread the sides of the cake with icing and do the top last.

Ingredients

100 g/4 oz margarine
1¾ cups/350 g/12 oz sugar
2 eggs
50 ml/2 floz red food coloring
2 Tbsp/30 g unsweetened cocoa
1¾ cup/250 g/9 oz plain flour
1 tsp salt
1 cup/225 ml/8 floz buttermilk
1 tsp vanilla extract
1 tsp bicarbonate of soda
1 tsp white wine vinegar

Icing

3 Tbsp flour
1¼ cup/225 g/8 oz sugar
1 cup/225 ml/8 floz milk
225 g/8 oz butter
1 tsp vanilla extract

BUTTERFLY CAKES

MAKES 14–16

INGREDIENTS

100 g/4 oz butter or margarine
½ cup/100 g/4 oz sugar
2 eggs
1 tsp grated orange zest
50 g/2 oz plain chocolate, finely grated
¾ cup/100 g/4 oz self-rising flour

Icing

75 g/3 oz butter or margarine
1 cup/175 g/6 oz confectioners sugar, sieved
75 g/3 oz plain chocolate, melted

To decorate

confectioners sugar
seedless raspberry jelly or candied cherries

Preheat the oven to 180°C/350°F. Put the butter or margarine and sugar into a bowl and cream together until light and fluffy.

Beat in the eggs a little at a time. Stir in the orange zest and chocolate.

Fold in the flour.

Arrange paper cases in a metal bun tin. Divide the mixture between the cases.

Bake in the oven for about 15–20 minutes. Cool.

To make the icing, cream together the butter and confectioners sugar. Gradually beat in the cooled, melted chocolate.

Starting ¼ inch/5 mm in from the edge, remove the top of each cake by cutting in and slightly down to form a cavity.

Pipe a little icing in the cavity of each cake.

Sprinkle the reserved cake tops with confectioners sugar and cut each one in half. Place each half, cut side outwards, on to the icing to form wings.

Pipe small rosettes of icing in the centre of each cake. Top with a small blob of raspberry jelly or half a candied cherry.

CHOCOLATE MERINGUES

MAKES 6–8

INGREDIENTS

3 egg whites
⅜ cup/75 g/3 oz caster sugar
75 g/3 oz confectioners sugar, sieved
¼ cup/25 g/1 oz unsweetened cocoa powder, sieved

Filling

⅔ cup/150 ml/¼ pt heavy cream
1 Tbsp soft brown sugar
2 tsp unsweetened cocoa powder

Preheat the oven to 110°C/225°F. Beat the egg whites until they form stiff peaks. Gradually whisk in the caster sugar, a little at a time.

Whisk in the confectioners sugar.

Fold in the cocoa powder.

Put the mixture into a piping bag fitted with a large star nozzle. Line baking sheets with greaseproof paper.

Pipe the mixture into spirals.

Bake in the oven for 2–3 hours or until the meringues are dry. Cool on a wire rack.

Whip the cream until stiff. Stir in the sugar and cocoa. Sandwich the meringues together, two at a time, with the chocolate cream.

CHOCOLATE-MINT CUP CAKES

MAKES ABOUT 18 TO 20

Preheat the oven to 180°C/350°F. Line 20 deep muffin or bun tins with paper cases.

Sift together the flour, bicarbonate of soda, salt and cocoa powder.

In a second large bowl, using an electric mixer, beat the butter and sugar until light and creamy, about 5 minutes. Add the eggs, 1 at a time, beating well after each addition, then beat in the mint essence.

On low speed, beat in the flour and cocoa mixture alternately with the milk just until blended. Spoon into paper cases, filling each tin about three-quarters full.

Bake for 12 to 15 minutes, until a fine skewer inserted in the centre comes out clean; do not overbake. Cool in the tins on a wire rack for 5 minutes; remove the cakes to a wire rack to cool completely.

Meanwhile, prepare the glaze. In a saucepan over low heat, melt the chocolate and butter, stirring until smooth. Remove from the heat and stir in the mint essence. Cool until spreadable, then spread on top of each cake.

INGREDIENTS

225 g/8 oz plain flour
1 tsp bicarbonate of soda
¼ tsp salt
50 g/2 oz cocoa powder
150 g/5 oz butter, softened
275 g/10 oz caster sugar
3 eggs
2 tsp peppermint essence
225 ml/8 fl oz milk

Chocolate-mint glaze

75 g/3 oz plain chocolate
50 g/2 oz butter
1 tsp peppermint essence

Chocolate Chip Cake

SERVES 8–12

Preheat the oven to 170°C/325°F. Cream the margarine and sugar until they are light and fluffy.

Add the nuts, flour, baking powder, egg yolks and the grated rind and juice of the orange. Mix well.

Fold in the chocolate pieces.

Whisk the egg whites until they are stiff but not dry. Gently fold into the cake mixture starting with just one spoonful and gradually adding the remainder.

Grease an 7 inch/18cm square cake pan and line with greaseproof paper.

Turn the mixture into the pan and bake for 45 minutes.

For a larger cake double all the ingredients and use a roasting pan, 9 x 11 inches/23 x 28 cm.

Ingredients

100 g/4 oz margarine

⅜ cup/75 g/3 oz soft brown sugar

100 g/4 oz ground hazelnuts

½ cup/75 g/3 oz plain flour

1 tsp baking powder

3 eggs, separated

1 orange

50 g/2 oz chocolate pieces

Chocolate Rum Cake

SERVES 6

Heat the water and sugar, stirring constantly, until the sugar has dissolved. Leave to cool.

Melt the chocolate in the top of a double boiler.

Add the cooled syrup, stirring constantly.

Stir in the rum, brandy or Grand Marnier and 3 tbsp cream.

Arrange half of the sponge fingers in the bottom of a serving dish.

Carefully sprinkle the coffee over the sponge fingers, enough to just moisten them.

Spread half of the chocolate mixture over the top.

Arrange a second layer of sponge fingers gently over the chocolate.

Sprinkle with coffee and spread with chocolate as before.

Whisk the remaining cream until it is just firm. Spread over the top of the cake (and the sides if you are using a flat plate), and chill for 1 hour.

Decorate with grated chocolate to serve.

Ingredients

1 Tbsp water
⅛ cup/25 g/1 oz sugar
100 g/4 oz plain chocolate in small pieces
15 ml/1 tbsp rum, brandy or Grand Marnier
1¼ cups/300 ml/½ pt heavy cream
20 sponge fingers (Boudoir biscuits)
⅓ cup/100 ml/4 floz cold black coffee
2 Tbsp grated chocolate

CHERRY CHOCOLATE CRUNCH

SERVES 8–10

Melt the chocolate with the butter in the top of a double boiler.

Lightly beat the egg and stir into the melted chocolate.

Combine all the ingredients and mix well so that the biscuit crumbs are well coated with chocolate.

Turn the chocolate mixture into a well greased 8 inch/20 cm cake pan.

Chill for at least 8 hours before serving.

INGREDIENTS

100 g/4 oz plain chocolate in small pieces
100 g/4 oz butter
1 egg
100 g/4 oz Graham cracker crumbs
50 g/2 oz candied cherries, chopped
¼ cup/50 ml/2 floz rum
2 Tbsp chopped nuts

Buche de Noël

SERVES 6–8

Preheat the oven to 230°C/450°F. Grease and line a 9 x 13 inch/23 x 33 cm Swiss roll tin.

Put the egg yolks and sugar into a mixing bowl and whisk until the mixture falls in a thick trail.

Whisk the egg whites until stiff.

Fold the egg whites and flour alternately into the egg yolk mixture. Pour into the tin and bake in the oven for about 10 minutes until golden brown.

Put a sheet of greaseproof paper on top of a dampened tea towel and sprinkle with caster sugar. Turn the sponge out on to the sugared paper.

Peel off the lining paper and quickly trim the edges of the sponge. Make a shallow groove across one short side of the cake 1 inch/2.5 cm from the edge.

Fold the sponge over at the groove. Using the towel as support, roll up the sponge with the greaseproof paper inside. Cover with the damp cloth until cold.

To make the butter cream, put the sugar and water into a small pan. Dissolve the sugar and then bring to the boil and boil to the "thread" stage 110°C/225°F.

Whisk the egg yolks in a bowl until thick and creamy. Slowly pour the hot syrup on to the egg yolks in a steady stream, beating constantly until the mixture is light and fluffy.

Beat the butter until soft. Add the egg mixture a little at a time until the mixture is firm and shiny. Stir in the chocolate and rum.

Carefully unroll the sponge and remove the greaseproof paper. Spread a little butter cream over the sponge and roll up again.

Put the cake on to a serving dish. Spoon the remaining butter cream into a piping bag fitted with a star nozzle. Pipe lines lengthways down the cake. Add an occasional swirl to represent a "knot" on a log.

Decorate with Meringue Mushrooms and marzipan, holly leaves and berries.

Ingredients

4 eggs, separated
½ cup/100 g/4 oz sugar
¾ cup/100 g/4 oz plain flour

Butter cream

⅜ cup/75 g/3 oz sugar
⅓ cup/85 ml/3 floz water
4 egg yolks
175 g/6 oz unsalted butter
75 g/3 oz plain chocolate, melted
5–10 ml/1–2 tsp dark rum

To decorate

Meringue Mushrooms (see page 157)
marzipan, holly leaves and berries

Chocolate-Chestnut Roulade

SERVES 12

Preheat the oven to 180°C/350°F. Grease the base and sides of a 15½ x 10½ x 1 inch/39 x 26 x 2.5 cm Swiss roll tin. Line the base with greaseproof paper, allowing 1 inch/2.5 cm to overhang; grease and flour the paper.

Melt the chocolate with the coffee, stirring frequently until smooth. Set aside.

Beat the egg yolks with half the sugar until pale and thick, about 5 minutes. Slowly beat in the chocolate just until blended.

In another large bowl; with an electric mixer, beat the egg whites and cream of tartar until stiff peaks form. Gradually sprinkle the sugar over the egg whites in 2 batches and continue beating until the egg whites are stiff and glossy; beat in the vanilla extract.

Stir 1 spoonful of egg whites into the chocolate mixture to lighten, then fold in the remaining egg whites. Spoon into the prepared tin, spreading evenly.

Bake for 12–15 minutes, or until the cake springs back when touched with a fingertip.

Meanwhile, dust a tea towel with cocoa powder. When the cake is done, turn out on to the towel immediately and remove the paper. Starting at a narrow end, roll the cake and towel together Swiss-roll fashion. Cool completely.

With an electric mixer, whip the cream and coffee-flavour liqueur or vanilla extract until soft peaks form. Beat 1 spoonful of cream into the chestnut purée to lighten, then fold in the remaining cream,

Unroll the cake and trim the edges. Spread the chestnut cream mixture to within 1 inch/2.5 cm of the edge of the cake. Using the towel to lift the cake, roll the cake.

Place the roulade seam-side down on a serving plate. Decorate the roulade with bands of sifted confectioners sugar and chopped marrons.

Ingredients

Roulade sponge

175 g/6 oz plain chocolate, chopped
½ cup/120 ml/4 floz strong coffee
6 eggs, separated
6 Tbsp caster sugar
½ tsp cream of tartar
2 tsp vanilla extract
cocoa powder for dusting

Chestnut cream filling

1¾ cups/450 ml/16 floz heavy cream
2 Tbsp coffee-flavour liqueur or
2 tsp vanilla extract
1¾ cups/475 ml/16 floz canned sweetened chestnut purée

To decorate

confectioners sugar
chopped marrons

Classic Devil's Food Cake

SERVES 10–12

Preheat the oven to 190°C/375°F. Butter 2 9 inch/23 cm round cake tins, 1½ inch/4 cm deep. Line the bottoms with greaseproof paper; butter the paper and flour the tins.

In the top of a double boiler over a low heat, melt the chocolate, stirring frequently until smooth. Set aside. Sift together the cocoa powder, flour, bicarbonate of soda and salt.

With an electric mixer, cream the butter, brown sugar and vanilla extract until light and creamy, about 5 minutes, scraping the side of the bowl occasionally. Add the eggs, 1 at a time, beating well after each addition.

Add the flour mixture alternately with the soured cream in 3 batches, beating until well blended. Stir in the vinegar and slowly beat in the boiling water; the batter will be thin. Pour into the tins.

Bake for 20–25 minutes, until a fine skewer inserted in the center comes out with just a few crumbs attached. Cool the cakes in tins on a wire rack. Remove the cakes from the tins. Remove from the paper and cool on a wire rack while preparing the icing.

In a saucepan over a medium heat, bring the cream to the boil. Remove from the heat and stir in the chocolate all at once until melted and smooth. Cool slightly. Pour into a large bowl and refrigerate for 1 hour, stirring twice, until the icing is spreadable.

With a serrated knife, slice each cake layer horizontally into 2 layers. Place 1 cake layer cut-side up on a cake plate and spread with one-sixth of the icing. Place a third layer on top and cover with another sixth of the icing, then cover with the fourth cake layer top-side (rounded) up. Ice top and sides of the cake with the remaining sugar. Serve at room temperature.

Ingredients

50 g/2 oz plain chocolate, chopped
65 g/2½ oz cocoa powder
250 g/9 oz plain flour
2 tsp bicarbonate of soda
½ tsp salt
150 g/ 5 oz unsalted butter; softened
425 g/15 oz soft brown sugar
1Tbsp vanilla extract
3 eggs
175 ml/6 floz soured cream
1 tsp vinegar
250 ml/8 floz boiling water
cocoa powder for dusting

Chocolate ganache icing

675 ml/24 floz whipping
675 g/1½ lb plain chocolate, chopped
1 Tbsp vanilla extract

Chapter Three

Pies and Pastries

TASTY PASTRY RECIPES
WITH A RANGE OF
FLAVORFUL INGREDIENTS

Chocolate Cream Pie

SERVES 8

Preheat the oven to 180°C/350°F. Lightly butter a 9 inch/23 cm, 1½ inch/4 cm deep pie dish or fluted baking dish.

In a food processor, process the chocolate cookies until fine crumbs form. Pour in the melted butter and process just until blended. Pat on to the bottom and sides of the pie dish.

Bake for 5–7 minutes, just until set. Transfer to a wire rack to cool completely.

In a saucepan over low heat, melt the chocolate with the whipping cream, stirring until smooth. Set aside.

In another saucepan, combine the cornstarch, flour and sugar. Gradually stir in the milk and cook over medium heat until thickened and bubbling.

In a bowl, beat the egg yolks lightly. Slowly pour 1 cup/250 ml/8 floz hot milk into the yolks, stirring constantly. Return the egg-yolk mixture to the pan and bring to a gentle boil, stirring constantly. Cook for 1 minute longer. Stir in the butter and melted chocolate until well blended. Pour into the prepared crust and place a piece of plastic wrap directly against the surface of the filling to prevent a skin forming. Cool, then refrigerate until completely chilled.

With an electric mixer, whip the cream until soft peaks form. In another bowl, with an electric mixer and clean blades, beat the egg whites and cream of tartar until stiff peaks form. Gradually sprinkle the sugar over in 2 batches, beating well after each addition, until the whites are stiff and glossy. Beat in the vanilla extract.

Fold 1 spoonful of egg white into the cream to lighten, then fold the remaining egg whites into the cream. Peel the plasticwrap from the chilled custard; spread the cream on to the custard in a swirling pattern. Dust the cream lightly with cocoa powder.

Ingredients

225 g/8 oz plain chocolate Graham crackers
50 g/2 oz butter, melted
175 g/6 oz plain chocolate, chopped
1 cup/250 ml/8 floz whipping cream
¼ cup/40 g/1½ oz cornstarch
1 tbsp plain flour
¼ cup/50 g/2 oz caster sugar
2¾ cups/675 ml/22 floz milk
5 egg yolks
40 g/1½ oz butter, softened

Light whipped cream

1½ cups/350 ml/12 floz heavy cream
2 egg whites
¼ tsp cream of tartar
¼ cup/50 g/2 oz sugar
2 tsp vanilla extract
cocoa powder for dusting

MISSISSIPPI MUD PIE

SERVES 8

Crush the cookies in a food processor or in a plastic bag with a rolling pin.

Stir in the butter and chocolate and mix well together.

Press the crumbs firmly and evenly over the bottom and sides of a greased 9 inch/23 cm flan dish. Chill.

Allow the ice creams to soften slightly. Put in a bowl and add the Tia Maria and brandy. Blend well together.

Spoon the ice cream into the chocolate case and put in the freezer until solid.

Remove the pie from the freezer about 15 minutes before serving. Decorate with whipped cream and grated chocolate.

INGREDIENTS

175 g/6 oz Graham crackers
large knob of butter, melted
100 g/4 oz plain chocolate, melted
5 cups/1.2 litres/2 pt coffee ice cream
5 cups/1.2 litres/2 pt chocolate ice cream
2 Tbsp Tia Maria
2 Tbsp brandy

To decorate

whipped cream
grated chocolate

CHOCOLATE AND PECAN PIE

SERVES 8–10

INGREDIENTS

1 cup/150 g/5 oz plain flour
1 tbsp caster sugar
½ tsp salt
100 g/4 oz small pieces butter
½ cup/120 ml/4 floz iced water

Filling

75 g/3 oz plain chocolate, chopped
25 g/1 oz butter, cut into pieces
3 eggs
¼ cup/50 g/2 oz light brown sugar
⅓ cup/75 ml/3 floz golden syrup
1 Tbsp vanilla extract
175 g/6 oz pecan halves
75 g/3 oz milk or plain chocolate chips (optional)

Prepare the piecrust. In a food processor fitted with a metal blade, process the flour, sugar and salt to blend. Add the butter and process for 15–20 seconds, until the mixture resembles coarse crumbs. With the machine running, add iced water through the feeder tube, just until the dough begins to stick together; do not allow the dough to form a ball or the pastry will be tough.

Turn the dough on to a floured work surface, shape into a flat disc and wrap tightly in plasticwrap. Refrigerate for 1 hour.

Lightly butter a 23 cm/9 inch pie dish, 1½ inch/4 cm deep. Soften the dough for 10–15 minutes at room temperature. On a well-floured surface, roll out the dough into a 12 inch/30 cm circle about ¼ inch/ 5 mm thick. Roll the dough loosely around the rolling pin and unroll over the pie dish; ease the dough into the dish.

With kitchen scissors, trim the dough, leaving about a ¼ inch/5 mmh overhang; flatten to the rim of the pie dish, pressing slightly towards the center of the dish. With a small knife, cut out hearts or other shapes from the dough trimmings. Brush the dough edge with water and press the dough shapes to the edge. Prick the bottom of dough with a fork. Refrigerate for 30 minutes.

Preheat the oven to 200°C/400°F. Line the pie shell with foil or greaseproof paper and fill with dry beans or rice. Bake for 5 minutes, then lift out foil or paper with the beans and bake for 5 minutes longer. Remove to a wire rack to cool slightly. Lower the oven temperature to 190°C/375°F.

In a saucepan over a low heat, melt the chocolate and butter, stirring until smooth. Set aside.

In a bowl, beat together the eggs, sugar, golden syrup and vanilla extract. Slowly beat in the melted chocolate. Sprinkle the pecan halves and chocolate chips (if using) over the bottom of the pastry. Place the pie dish on a baking sheet and carefully pour in the chocolate mixture.

Bake for 35–40 minutes, until the chocolate mixture is set; the top may crack slightly. If the pastry edges begin to overbrown, cover with strips of foil. Transfer to a wire rack to cool. Serve warm with softly whipped cream.

White Chocolate Mousse and Strawberry Tart

SERVES 10–12

Prepare the pastry. In a bowl, with a hand-held electric mixer, beat the butter; sugar and salt until creamy, about 2 minutes. Add the egg yolks and vanilla extract and beat until smooth. Add half the flour to the mixture, then stir in the remaining flour by hand until well blended.

Place a piece of plasticwrap on a work surface. Scrape the dough on to the plasticwrap. Use to help shape the dough into a flat disc and wrap tightly. Refrigerate for 1 hour.

Lightly butter a 10 inch/25 cm tart tin with a removable base. Soften the dough for 10 minutes at room temperature. On a well-floured surface, roll out the dough to a 11½–12 inch/28–30 cm circle about ⅛ inch/3 mm thick. Roll the dough loosely around the rolling pin and unroll over the tart tin. Ease the dough into the tin, patching if necessary.

With floured fingers, press the overhang down slightly toward the center, making the top edge thicker. Cut off the excess dough. Press the thicker top edge against the side of the tin to form a rim about 5 mm/¼ inch higher than the tin. Using your thumb and forefinger, crimp the edge. Prick the bottom of the dough with a fork. Refrigerate for 1 hour.

Preheat the oven to 190°C/375°F. Line the tart shell with foil or greaseproof paper; fill with dry beans or rice. Bake for 10 minutes; lift out the foil or paper with the beans and bake for 5–7 minutes longer until set and golden. Remove to a wire rack to cool completely.

Prepare the strawberry filling. Cut the strawberries in half lengthwise. In a bowl, mash about 350 g/12 oz strawberry halves with the cherry-flavor liqueur. Set the remaining berries and the mashed berries aside.

Prepare the mousse. In a saucepan over a low heat, melt the white chocolate with the cherry-flavor liqueur, water and ½ cup/120 ml/4 floz cream, stirring until smooth. Set aside to cool.

With an electric mixer, beat the remaining cream until soft peaks form. Stir 1 spoonful of cream into the chocolate mixture to lighten, then fold in the remaining cream. If you like, beat the egg whites with the cream of tartar until stiff peaks form then fold them into the chocolate cream mixture to make a lighter, softer mousse.

Pour about one-third of the mousse mixture into the cooled tart shell. Spread the mashed berries evenly over the mousse, then cover with the remaining mousse mixture.

To serve, arrange the sliced strawberries cut side up in concentric circles around the tart to cover the mousse. Remove the side of the tin and slide the tart onto a serving plate. Spoon the melted white chocolate into a paper cone and drizzle the white chocolate over the tart; alternatively, decorate the center with white chocolate curls, or glaze with seedless strawberry jam.

Ingredients

100 g/4 oz butter, softened
¼ cup/50 g/2 oz caster sugar
½ tsp salt
3 egg yolks
1 tsp vanilla extract
1 cup/150 g/5 oz plain flour

Strawberry filling

900 g/2 lb fresh, ripe strawberries
2 Tbsp cherry-flavour liqueur

White chocolate mousse filling

250 g/9 oz white chocolate, chopped
3 Tbsp cherry-flavor liqueur
2 Tbsp water
1½ cup cups/350 ml/12 floz heavy cream
2 egg whites (optional)
¼ tsp cream of tartar (optional)

To decorate

25 g/1 oz white chocolate, melted, or white chocolate curls (see page 12/13)
2 Tbsp seedless strawberry jam, melted and cooled

Rich Chocolate Meringue Pie

SERVES 6

Preheat the oven to 200°C/400°F, Gas Mark 6). Crush the cookies until they resemble fine breadcrumbs.

Melt the butter and stir into the cookies. Press the cookies over the base and sides of a 8 inch/20 cm ovenproof flan dish.

Blend together the sugar, flour, cornstarch, egg yolks and a little of the milk. Heat the remaining milk.

Stir the hot milk on to the flour mixture and whisk well. Return the mixture to the pan. Heat gently, stirring until the mixture thickens.

Stir in the butter, chocolate and rum if used. Stir until smooth. Pour into the cookie pie shell. Chill.

About 30 minutes before serving, make the meringue topping. Whisk the egg whites until stiff.

Whisk in half the sugar a teaspoonful at a time. Add the remaining sugar and whisk well.

Spread the meringue over the chocolate flan. Swirl decoratively with a teaspoon.

Bake in the oven for 3–5 minutes, until the meringue is golden brown.

Sprinkle with a little ground cinnamon.

Ingredients

225 g/8 oz Graham crackers
100 g/4 oz butter

Filling

⅛ cup/25 g/1 oz sugar
⅛ cup/25 g/1 oz plain flour
2 level tsp cornstarch
2 egg yolks
1⅔ cups/300 ml/½ pt milk
25 g/1 oz butter
100 g/4 oz plain chocolate, finely chopped
2 tsp rum (optional)

Topping

2 egg whites
½ cup/100g/4 oz caster sugar
ground cinnamon

Black-Bottom Lemon Tartlets

MAKES 12

Ingredients

1¼ cups/175 g /6 oz plain flour
2 Tbsp confectioners sugar
½ tsp salt
175 g/6 oz unsalted butter, cut into pieces and at room temperature
1 egg yolk
2.5 ml/½ tsp vanilla extract
2–3 Tbsp cold water

Lemon custard sauce

1 lemon
1½ cups/350 ml/12 floz milk
6 egg yolks
⅓ cup/75 g/3 oz sugar

Lemon curd filling

2 lemons
175 g/6 oz unsalted butter, cut into pieces
1⅛ cups/225 g/8 oz sugar
3 eggs

Chocolate filling

¾ cups/175 ml/6 floz cream
175 g/6 oz plain chocolate, chopped
25 g/1 oz unsalted butter, cut into pieces

To decorate

Chocolate triangles (see page 12/13)
25 g/1 oz plain chocolate, melted

First prepare the custard sauce. With a vegetable peeler, remove strips of zest from the lemon. Place in a saucepan over medium heat with the milk and bring to the boil. Remove from the heat and leave for 5 minutes. Reheat the milk gently.

Beat the egg yolks and sugar until pale and thick, 2–3 minutes. Pour about 1 cup/250 ml/8 floz hot milk over, beating vigorously. Return the mixture to the pan and cook gently over a low heat until it thickens; do not let it boil. Strain into a chilled bowl. Squeeze 2 tbsp lemon juice and stir into the sauce. Cool, stirring occasionally. Refrigerate until needed.

Prepare the lemon curd filling. Grate the zest and squeeze the juice of the lemons into the top of a double boiler. Add butter and sugar and stir over medium heat until butter is melted and sugar dissolved. Lower the heat. In a bowl, lightly beat the eggs, then string into the butter mixture. Cook over a low heat, stirring until mixture thickens, about 15 minutes. Pour (or strain if you do not want the lemon zest) into a bowl. Cool, stirring occasionally. Refrigerate to thicken.

Prepare the pastry. Place flour, sugar and salt into a food processor with a metal blade. Process to blend. Add the butter and process for 15–20 seconds, until the mixture resembles coarse crumbs. In a bowl, beat the egg yolk; vanilla extract and water. With the processor running, pour the egg yolk mixture through the feed tube until the dough begins to stick together; do not allow the dough to form a ball or the pastry will be tough. If the dough appears too dry add 1–2 tbsp water.

Place a piece of plasticwrap on a work surface. Turn the dough out on to the plasticwrap and shape the dough into a flat disc. Wrap tightly and refrigerate for at least 30 minutes.

Lightly butter 3 inch/12 7.5 cm tartlet tins. On a lightly floured surface, roll out the dough to an oblong shape slightly more than ⅛ inch/3 mm thick. Using a 4 inch/10 cm fluted cutter, cut out 12 circles and press each on to the bottom and sides of the tins. Prick the bottom of the dough with a fork. Place the tins on a large baking sheet and refrigerate for 30 minutes.

Preheat the oven to 190°C/375°F. Cut out 12 5 inch/12.5 cm circles of foil and line each tin; fill with dry beans. Bake for 5–8 minutes; remove the foil and beans and bake for 5 minutes, until golden. Transfer to a wire rack to cool.

Prepare the chocolate filling. In a saucepan over a medium heat, bring the cream to the boil. Remove from the heat and stir in the chocolate until melted and smooth. Beat in the butter and leave to cool slightly.

Spoon an equal amount of chocolate filling into each tartlet. Refrigerate for 10 minutes.

On to each chocolate-filled tartlet,

spoon on a layer of lemon curd. Set aside, but do not refrigerate. Spoon a little custard on to dessert plates. Remove the tartlets from the tins and place in the center of the plates. Decorate each tartlet with a chocolate triangle.

Chocolate Chiffon Pie

SERVES 6–8

Preheat the oven to 190°C/375°F. Roll out the pastry and use to line a 8 inch/20 cm flan tin. Bake "blind" (lined with greaseproof paper and baking beans) in the oven for 20–25 minutes. Remove the greaseproof paper and baking beans and return to the oven for a further 5–10 minutes until crisp and lightly browned. Leave to cool.

Put the milk, ½ oz/25 g sugar and chocolate into a saucepan and melt over a gentle heat. Stir continuously. Cool slightly.

Whisk the egg yolks into the chocolate mixture.

Dissolve the gelatin in the water and stir into the chocolate. Leave until the mixture is beginning to thicken and set.

Whisk the egg whites until stiff. Whisk in the remaining sugar.

Whisk the cream until it stands in soft peaks.

Fold the egg whites and cream thoroughly into the chocolate mixture. Pour into the pastry case. Chill until set.

To serve, pipe whipped cream over the top and pipe chocolate curls in the center.

Ingredients

175 g/6 oz shortcrust pastry
⅔ cup/150 ml/¼ pt milk
⅓ cup/75 g/3 oz sugar
100 g/4 oz plain chocolate, chopped
2 small eggs, separated
2 tsp powdered gelatin
2 Tbsp water
⅔ cup/150 ml/¼ pt heavy cream

To decorate

whipped cream
chocolate curls (see pages 12/13)

Chapter Four

Cold Desserts

ICE CREAMS, MOUSSES,
YOGURTS AND OTHER
DELICIOUS COLD DISHES FOR
HOT SUMMER DAYS

Chocolate Tiramisù

SERVES 14–16

Prepare the sponge fingers. Grease 2 large baking sheets and line with greaseproof paper. Grease and lightly flour the paper. In a bowl, sift together twice the flour, cocoa powder, coffee powder and salt. Mix well and set aside.

In another bowl, with an electric mixer, beat the egg yolks with ¼ cup/50 g/2 oz sugar until thick and pale, 2–3 minutes. Beat in the vanilla extract.

In a large bowl, with an electric mixer, beat the egg whites and cream of tartar until stiff peaks form. Sprinkle over the remaining sugar, 2 tbsp at a time, beating well after each addition.

Fold 1 spoonful of egg whites into the egg-yolk mixture to lighten, then fold in remaining egg whites. Sift the flour mixture over and fold into the egg mixture, but do not overwork. Spoon the batter into a large piping bag fitted with a medium (about ½ inch/1 cm) plain nozzle. Pipe the batter into about 30 5 inch/12.5 cm or 24 4 inch/10 cm sponge fingers. Dust with confectioners sugar.

Bake for 12–15 minutes, until set and tops feel firm when touched with a finger-tip. Transfer to a wire rack to cool on baking sheets for 10 minutes. With a wide spatula, transfer the sponge fingers to wire racks to cool.

With a hand-held electric mixer at low speed, beat the mascarpone cheese with the confectioners sugar just until smooth. Gradually beat in ¼ cup/60 ml/2 floz coffee; do not overbeat.

In another bowl, with an electric mixer, beat the cream until soft peaks form. Gently fold the cream into the mascar-pone mixture. Divide the mixture in half. Fold the melted chocolate and 2 tbsp coffee-flavor liqueur into half until blended. Fold the grated chocolate and chocolate-flavor liqueur into the remain-ing mascarpone mixture. Set both mixtures aside.

In a bowl or pie dish wide enough to hold the sponge fingers, combine half the remaining instant coffee with 30 ml/2 tbsp coffee-flavor liqueur. Quickly dip side of a sponge finger into the coffee mixture and place it dry-side down in a 13 x 9 inch/32.5 x 23 cm baking dish; do not let the sponge fingers get too soggy. Continue with about half the sponge fingers (you will need enough for 2 layers) to form a fairly close layer with not much space between each finger. Place the remaining coffee and coffee-flavor liqueur in the pie dish.

Pour the chocolate-mascarpone mixture over the bottom layer of sponge fingers, smoothing the chocolate mixture. Layer the remaining sponge fingers over the chocolate mixture 1 at a time. Drizzle over any remaining coffee mixture. Pour the grated chocolate-mascarpone mixture over this layer and smooth the top, layer no spaces between filling and sides of dish. Cover the dish tightly and refriger-ate overnight. Dust the top with cocoa powder before serving.

Ingredients

Chocolate sponge fingers

½ cup/75 g/3 oz plain flour
⅓ cup/25 g/1 oz cocoa powder
1 Tbsp instant coffee powder
¼ tsp salt
4 eggs, separated
½ cup/100 g/4 oz caster sugar
2 tsp vanilla extract
¼ tsp cream of tartar
confectioners sugar for dusting

Chocolate mascarpone filling

490 g/17½ oz container mascarpone cheese, at room temperature
⅓ cup/75 g/3 oz confectioners sugar, sifted
1½ cup/350 ml/12 floz freshly brewed instant coffee
2½ cup/600 ml/1 pt heavy cream
175 g/6 oz plain chocolate, melted and cooled
90 ml/6 tbsp coffee-flavor liqueur
50 g/2 oz plain chocolate, grated
2 Tbsp chocolate-flavor liqueur

To serve

cocoa powder for dusting
whipped cream (optional)

Rich Mocha Refridgerator Cake

SERVES 8

This delicious dessert cake is based on an Italian recipe. It combines the strong taste of espresso coffee with the sweetness of chocolate.

Line a 2-pound loaf tin with non-stick baking parchment. Melt the chocolate in a large bowl over hot water. Dissolve the instant espresso in the hot water, then add it to the melted chocolate with the liqueur. Stir until thoroughly blended. Leave to cool slightly.

Beat the butter in a bowl until soft, then add the sugar and egg yolks, one at a time. Stir in the almonds and cooled chocolate. Whisk the egg whites until stiff, then fold them into the mixture. Carefully add the cookie halves one at a time, tossing them gently until they are coated with chocolate. Make sure they remain separate and do not stick together.

Carefully spoon the mixture into the prepared pan, pressing down lightly to ensure there are no gaps, but avoid breaking the cookies. Try to ensure that the cookies are evenly distributed throughout the loaf. Chill for at least 2 hours.

To serve, turn the loaf out onto a serving plate and remove the paper. Sprinkle with sieved confectioner's sugar, if you wish, and serve in slices. Keep the cake chilled until you are ready to serve.

TIP

This cake is very rich and should be served with just a small dollop of sweetened yogurt. Omit the eggs if you prefer, for a slightly heavier cake, which is still utterly delicious.

Ingredients

300 g/10 oz dark chocolate, broken into small pieces
2 Tbsp instant espresso
½ cup/120 ml/4 floz hot water
3 Tbsp Tia Maria or other coffee liqueur
50 g/2 oz unsalted butter
2 Tbsp superfine sugar
2 eggs, separated
1 cup/220 g /8 oz roughly chopped blanched almonds
12 butter cookies, cut cleanly into halves
Confectioner's sugar (optional)

Chocolate Pavlova

with Kiwi Fruit and Orange

SERVES 8–10

Preheat the oven to 170°C/325°F. Place a sheet of greaseproof paper on a large baking sheet and mark a 8 inch/20 cm circle on it using a plate or cake tin as a guide. Into a bowl, sift together the cocoa powder and cornstarch; set aside.

In another bowl, with an electric mixer, beat the egg whites until frothy. Add the salt and continue beating until stiff peaks form. Sprinkle in the sugar, 1 tbsp at a time, making sure each addition is well blended before adding the next, until stiff and glossy. Fold in the cocoa and cornstarch mixture, then fold in the vinegar.

Spoon the mixture on to the circle on the paper, spreading the meringue evenly and building up the sides higher than the center. Bake in the center of the oven for 45–50 minutes, until set. Turn off the oven and leave the meringue to stand in the oven 45 minutes longer; the meringue may crack or sink.

Meanwhile, prepare the chocolate cream. In a saucepan over low heat, melt the chocolate with the milk, stirring until smooth. Beat in the butter and cool completely.

Remove the meringue from the oven. Using a palette knife, transfer to a serving plate. Cut a circle around the center of the meringue about 2 inches/5 cm from the edge; this allows the center to sink gently without pulling the edges in.

When the chocolate mixture is completely cool, in a bowl, with an electric mixer, beat the cream until soft peaks form. Stir half the cream into the chocolate to lighten, then fold in the remaining cream. Spoon into the center of the meringue.

Arrange the kiwi fruit and orange in the center of the chocolate cream and decorate with fresh mint and wallflowers.

Ingredients

3 tbsp cocoa powder
1 tsp cornstarch
4 egg whites, at room temperature
¼ tsp salt
1¼ cups/225 g/8 oz caster sugar
1 tsp cider vinegar

White chocolate cream

100 g/4 oz good-quality white chocolate, chopped
½ cup/120 ml/4 floz milk
15 g/½ oz unsalted butter, cut into pieces
1 cup/250 ml/8 floz heavy cream
2 kiwi fruit, peeled and sliced
2 oranges, segmented

To decorate

fresh mint sprigs, wallflowers

Chocolate Frozen Yogurt

SERVES 4–6

Ingredients

5 cups/1.2 litres/2 pt plain low-fat yogurt
1½ cups/300 g/11 oz sugar
½ cup/75 g/3 oz cocoa powder
1 Tbsp skimmed milk powder, dissolved in
1–2 Tbsp milk or water

In a bowl, with a wire whisk, mix together the yogurt, sugar, cocoa and dissolved skimmed milk powder until smooth and well blended and the sugar is dissolved. Refrigerate for 1 hour, until cold.

Transfer the yogurt mixture to an ice-cream maker and freeze according to the manufacturer's instructions; this mixture will not freeze as hard as ice cream. Transfer to a freezerproof serving bowl or container and freeze for 3–4 hours, until firm. (Frozen yogurt can be stored in the freezer for 2–3 weeks in a freezerproof container.)

VARIATION

For mocha frozen yogurt, use coffee-flavor low-fat yogurt and add 1 tbsp instant coffee powder, or experiment with other flavors.

Chocolate Mousse

SERVES 4–6

Ingredients

175 g/6 oz plain chocolate
2 Tbsp honey
3 eggs, separated
⅛ cup/15 g/½ oz powdered gelatin
45 ml/3 tbsp hot water
⅔ cup/150 ml/¼ pt heavy cream

To serve

whipped cream
sliced bananas

Put the chocolate and honey into a bowl over a pan of hot water and melt.

Stir in the egg yolks and beat until smooth. Remove from the heat.

Dissolve the gelatin in the water. Stir into the chocolate mixture. Chill until the mixture is the consistency of unbeaten egg white.

Whip the cream until thick, but not stiff. Fold into the chocolate mixture.

Whisk the egg whites until stiff and fold them into the chocolate mixture.

Pour into a 4 cups/1 litre/1¾ pt mold. Chill until set.

Unmold on to a serving dish. Pipe whipped cream round the base and decorate with banana slices.

PROFITEROLES

SERVES 6

INGREDIENTS

50 g/2 oz unsalted butter
⅔ cup/150 ml/¼ pt water
½ cup/65 g/2½ oz plain flour
2 eggs, beaten

Filling

1¼ cup/300 ml/½ pt heavy cream
⅛ cup/25 g/1 oz confectioners sugar, sieved
a little Grand Marnier
2 tsp finely-grated orange zest

Chocolate sauce

100 g/4 oz plain chocolate
30 ml/2 Tbsp orange juice
¼ cup/50 g/2 oz confectioners sugar
25 g/1 oz butter

Melt the butter in a pan with the water.

Bring to the boil and immediately tip in the flour. Beat well until the mixture forms a ball that comes cleanly away from the pan. Leave to cool.

Preheat the oven to 200°C/400°F. Beat or whisk the eggs into the mixture, a little at a time. Continue beating until the mixture is smooth and glossy.

Put the mixture into a piping bag fitted with a ½ inch/1 cm plain nozzle. Pipe about 24 small balls on to a greased and floured baking sheet.

Bake in the oven for 15–20 minutes until well risen and golden brown. A few minutes before removing from the oven, pierce them with a sharp knife to release the steam. Cool on a wire rack.

To make the filling, whisk the cream until stiff. Stir in the confectioners sugar, Grand Marnier and orange zest. Put the cream in a piping bag fitted with a small nozzle and pipe the cream into the choux buns through the slits.

To make the sauce, put all the ingredients into a bowl over a pan of hot water and heat until melted. Stir well together.

Pile the profiteroles on a serving dish and just before serving, pour over the warm sauce.

Chocolate and Strawberry Frozen Daquoise

SERVES 10

Preheat the oven to 140°C/275°F. Line 1 large and 1 small baking sheet with greaseproof paper or foil. Using a 8 inch/ 20 cm cake tin or plate as a guide, mark 2 circles on the large baking sheet and 1 circle on the small baking sheet.

In a bowl, mix together ¼ cup/50 g/2 oz) sugar and the cocoa powder. Set aside.

With an electric mixer, beat the egg whites and cream of tartar until stiff peaks form. Gradually sprinkle the remaining sugar over, a little at a time, beating well after each addition, until the egg whites are stiff and glossy. Gently fold in the cocoa and sugar mixture just until blended.

Spoon one-third of the meringue mixture inside each marked circle on the baking sheets. Spread each meringue out evenly to a 8 inch/20 cm circle, smoothing the tops and edges.

Bake the meringues for 1¼ hours, until crisp and dry. Transfer to wire racks to cool for 10 minutes on baking sheets. Then remove the meringues from the greaseproof paper or foil to cool completely; the meringues can be stored in an airtight container if they are not to be used at once.

Place the meringue layers on a freezer-proof serving plate and freeze for 20 minutes; this makes them firmer and easier to handle while spreading the ice cream. Meanwhile, remove the chocolate and strawberry ice creams from the freezer to soften for 15–20 minutes.

Remove the meringue layers and serving plate from the freezer., Place 1 meringue layer on the plate and spread with chocolate ice cream to within ½ inch/1 cm of the edge. Cover with a second meringue layer and spread with strawberry ice cream to within ½ inch/ 1 cm of the edge. Top with the third meringue layer, pressing the layers gently together. Return to the freezer for 5–6 hours or overnight.

In a bowl, with a hand-held mixer, beat the cream, sugar and raspberry-flavor liqueur until soft peaks form. Remove the meringue layers from the freezer and spread the top and side with cream in a swirling or decorative pattern. Freeze until ready to serve if not using at once.

For the sauce, process the strawberries in a food processor with a metal blade attached, until well blended. Press the purée through a sieve into a bowl. Stir in the lemon juice and if the sauce is too thick, thin with a little water.

To serve, slice fresh strawberries lengthwise and decorate the top of the daquoise. Serve each slice with some strawberry sauce and a chocolate-dipped strawberry.

Ingredients

1½ cups/275 g/10 oz sugar
2 Tbsp cocoa powder, sifted
5 egg whites
¼ tsp cream of tartar
2½ cups/600 ml/1 pt good-quality chocolate ice cream
600 ml/1 pt good-quality strawberry ice cream
2 cups/475 ml/16 floz whipping cream
¼ cup/50 g/2 oz sugar
30 ml/2 Tbsp raspberry-flavor liqueur

Strawberry sauce

450 g/1 lb frozen strawberries, drained
15 ml/1 Tbsp lemon juice

To decorate

350 g/12 oz fresh strawberries
10 chocolate-dipped strawberries (p171)

INGREDIENTS

225 g/8 oz plain chocolate, chopped
2 cups475 ml/16 floz half cream or milk
3 egg yolks
¼ cup/50 g/2 oz sugar
1½ cups/350 ml/12 floz heavy cream
15 ml/1 Tbsp vanilla extract

RICH CHOCOLATE ICE CREAM

SERVES 4

In a saucepan over a low heat, melt the chocolate with ½ cup/120 ml/4 floz half cream or milk, stirring frequently until smooth. Remove from the heat.

In a saucepan over a medium heat, bring the remaining half cream or milk to the boil. In a bowl, with a hand-held mixer, beat the egg yolks and sugar until thick and creamy, 2–3 minutes. Gradually pour the hot milk over the egg yolks, beating constantly, then return the mixture to the saucepan.

Cook over medium heat until the custard thickens and lightly coats the back of a wooden spoon, stirring constantly; do not let the mixture boil or the custard will curdle. Immediately pour the melted chocolate over, stirring constantly until well blended.

Pour the cold cream into a bowl and strain custard into the bowl with the cream. Blend well and cool to room temperature. Refrigerate until cold.

Transfer the custard to an ice-cream maker and freeze according to the manufacturer's instructions. Leave to soften for 15–20 minutes.

VARIATIONS

White, Dark or Milk Chocolate Chunk: Stir 225 g/8 oz good-quality white, dark or milk chocolate, chopped, into the ice cream when removing from the ice-cream maker.

Mocha Ice Cream: Prepare the ice cream as directed but add 2 tbsp instant coffee powder, dissolved in 2 tbsp water, to the melted chocolate before adding to the custard.

Fruited White Chocolate Bavarian Creams
with Passion Fruit and Chocolate Sauces

SERVES 8

Lightly oil 8 heart-shaped or other molds. In a saucepan over low heat, bring ⅔ cup/150 ml/5 floz cream to the boil. Add the white chocolate all at once, stirring until smooth. Set aside.

Sprinkle the gelatin over the water in a bowl; leave to stand and soften.

In a saucepan over a medium heat, bring the milk to the boil. In a bowl with a hand-held electric mixer, beat the egg yolks and sugar until thick and pale, 2–3 minutes. Reduce the mixer to the lowest speed, gradually beat in the milk, then return the custard mixture to the saucepan.

Cook the custard over a medium heat, stirring constantly with a wooden spoon until the mixture thickens and coats the back of the spoon; do not boil or the custard will curdle. Remove from the heat and stir in the softened gelatin until dissolved, then stir into the chocolate mixture. Strain the custard into a large chilled bowl. Stir in the orange-flavor liqueur and refrigerate for about 20 minutes, until the mixture begins to thicken.

In a bowl, with an electric mixer, beat the remaining cream until soft peaks form. Gently fold into the thickening gelatin-custard mixture. Spoon an equal amount into each mold. Place the molds on a baking sheet and refrigerate for 2 hours, or until set. Cover all the molds with plasticwrap and refrigerate for several hours.

Prepare the passion fruit sauce. Halve the passion fruit crosswise. Scoop the juice and seeds into a saucepan. Stir in the orange juice, sugar and dissolved cornstarch. Bring to the boil, then simmer for 1–2 minutes, until the sauce thickens. Remove from the heat; cool slightly. Stir in the orange-flavor liqueur. Pour into a sauceboat.

Prepare the chocolate sauce. In a saucepan over a medium heat, melt the chocolate and butter with water, stirring frequently until smooth. Remove from the heat and cool slightly. Stir in the chocolate-flavor liqueur and strain into a sauceboat.

To serve, unmold the desserts on to plates at least 30 minutes before serving to soften slightly. Fill a pie dish with hot water. Run a knife around the edge of each mold and dip into the hot water for 5–7 seconds. Dry the bottom of the mold; quickly cover the dessert with a plate. Invert the mold on to the plate giving a firm shake; carefully remove the mold.

Spoon a little of each sauce around each heart-shaped Bavarian cream. Decorate with grated chocolate and fresh mint.

Ingredients

vegetable oil for molds
1⅓ cup/325 ml/11 floz whipping cream
100 g/4 oz good-quality white chocolate, chopped
2 tsp powdered gelatin
¼ cup/60 ml/2 floz water
2 cups/450 ml/16 floz milk
4 egg yolks
50 g/2 oz sugar
2 Tbsp orange-flavor liqueur

Passion fruit sauce

6 very ripe passion fruit
¼ cup/60 ml/2 floz orange juice
2 Tbsp sugar or to taste
1 tsp cornstarch, dissolved in 1 tsp water
1 Tbsp orange-flavor liqueur

Chocolate liqueur sauce

225 g/8 oz bittersweet chocolate, chopped
50 g/2 oz unsalted butter, cut into pieces
¾ cup/175 ml/6 floz water
2–3 Tbsp chocolate-flavor liqueur

To decorate

grated chocolate
fresh mint sprigs

CHARLOTTE LOUISE

SERVES 8

INGREDIENTS

18–20 sponge fingers
175 g/76 oz unsalted butter
½ cup/75 g/3 oz sugar
175 g/6 oz plain chocolate
100 g/4 oz ground almonds
1¼ cup/300 ml/½ pt heavy cream
2.5 ml/½ tsp almond extract

To decorate

whipped cream
pistachio nuts
candied violets or roses
satin ribbon

Cut a round of greaseproof paper to fit the base of a 6 cups/1.4 litre/2½ pt charlotte mold. Oil it lightly and place in the mold.

Line the sides of the mold with the sponge fingers.

Cream the butter and sugar together until light and fluffy.

Melt the chocolate. Cool slightly, then beat into the butter together with the ground almonds.

Whip the cream until thick, but not stiff. Add the almond extract. Fold into the chocolate mixture and mix well.

Spoon the mixture into the lined mold. Press in firmly. Chill well.

Turn out on to a plate. Remove the paper and pipe with whipped cream. Decorate with pistachio nuts and candied violets or roses. Tie a satin ribbon around the charlotte.

PEARS AND CHOCOLATE SAUCE

SERVES 6

INGREDIENTS

100 g/4 oz plain chocolate
2 Tbsp strong black coffee
2 Tbsp apricot jelly
3 Tbsp water
4 Tbsp heavy cream
large pinch of ground cinnamon
4–8 scoops vanilla or chocolate ice cream
6 ripe pears, peeled, halved and cored
crisp cookies (such as *Langues de chat*), to serve

Put the chocolate, coffee, jelly and water into a small heavy pan. Slowly bring to the boil, stirring constantly.

Remove from the heat and stir in the cream and cinnamon.

Sieve into a bowl and leave to cool.

Put 1 or 2 scoops of ice cream in 6 individual serving dishes. Arrange 2 pear halves on each serving.

Spoon over the chocolate sauce and serve immediately with crisp cookies.

White Chocolate Fruit Fools in Chocolate Cups

SERVES 12

Ingredients

12 chocolate cups (see page 189)

Mango purée

1 mango, peeled and cut into cubes, with 4 cubes reserved for decoration
grated zest and juice of ½ orange
1 tsp lemon juice or to taste
1 Tbsp sugar or to taste

Kiwi fruit purée

3 kiwi fruit, peeled and sliced, with 4 slices reserved for decoration
grated zest of 1 lime with 1–2 tsp juice
1 Tbsp sugar or to taste

Cranberry-raspberry purée

100 g/4 oz fresh raspberries with berries reserved for garnish
1 Tbsp lemon juice
1 tsp sugar or to taste
225 g/8 oz can cranberry sauce

White chocolate mousse

100 g/4 oz good-quality white chocolate, chopped
¼ cup/60 ml/2 floz milk
15 ml/1Tbsp orange-flavor liqueur
1¼ cups/300 ml/10 floz heavy cream
2 egg whites
¼ tsp cream of tartar

Prepare chocolate cups as directed on page 189, using 1½ lb/675 g plain chocolate and 1 tbsp white vegetable fat and extra-large paper cases.

Prepare the fruit purées in a blender, beginning with the lightest color purée to avoid washing the processor after each purée. Place the mango cubes in the processor with the orange zest and juice. Process until smooth. Taste and add lemon juice and sugar if necessary; this depends on the natural sweetness of the fruit. Scrape into a bowl. Cover and refrigerate.

Place the kiwi slices into the processor with lime zest and juice. Process until smooth. Taste and add more lime juice and sugar if necessary. Scrape into a bowl. Cover and refrigerate.

Place the raspberries, lemon juice and sugar into the processor. Process until smooth. Press through a strainer into a bowl. Return to the food processor. Add the cranberry sauce and using the pulse action, process once or twice, just to blend, but leaving some texture to the purée. Taste and add more lemon juice or sugar if necessary. Scrape the purée into small bowl. Cover and refrigerate.

Prepare the mousse. In a saucepan over low heat, melt the white chocolate with the milk, stirring frequently until smooth. Remove from the heat and stir in the orange-flavor liqueur. Cool to room temperature.

With a hand-held electric mixer, beat the cream until soft peaks form. Stir 1 spoonful of cream into the chocolate mixture to lighten, then fold in the remaining cream.

In another bowl, with an electric mixer, beat egg whites and cream of tartar until stiff peaks form. Fold into the chocolate-cream mixture. (You may not want to use all the egg whites if the mousse is soft enough; Divide into 3 bowls.

To assemble, arrange the prepared chocolate cups on 1 large or 2 smaller baking sheets (arrange adequate refrigerator space beforehand). Spoon a little of the mango purée into 4 chocolate cups. Spoon a little of the raspberry purée into 4 chocolate cups and then the kiwi fruit purée into the remaining 4 cups. Reserve a little of each purée for topping, then fold each of the purées into one of each of the 3 bowls of mousse; do not mix well – leave swirls of purée visible for effect. Spoon each fool mixture into the appropriate chocolate cups and top each with a decorative swirl of its matching purée. Refrigerate until ready to serve. Decorate each with a berry or a cube or slice of fruit. Refrigerate for at least 30 minutes or until firm.

DOUBLE CHOCOLATE PEPPERMINT

A chocolate and peppermint treat that can be made even more special by adding 1 to 2 tablespoons of crème de menthe, if you wish.

Blend the cocoa and sugar to a thin paste with a little of the cold milk, then add the remaining milk. Heat the remaining milk until almost boiling, add the sugar and stir until dissolved, then add the vanilla flavoring to the hot milk. Add the crème de menthe to the milk when completely cold, if desired.

Freeze-church until thick, then add the chopped peppermint creams and the chocolate chips. Continue to churn until the ice milk is ready to serve.

INGREDIENTS

3 Tbsp unsweetened cocoa powder, sieved
125 g/4½ oz caster sugar
600 ml/1 pint milk
1 tsp vanilla extract, or 2 tsp vanilla essence
1-2 Tbsp crème de menthe (optional)
50 g/1¾ oz peppermint creams, chopped
25 g/1 oz chocolate chips, roughly cut

Triple Chocolate Mousse Parfaits

SERVES 6

First prepare the bittersweet chocolate mousse. In a saucepan, melt the chocolate with cream, stirring frequently until smooth. Remove from the heat. Stir in the butter and beat in the egg yolks, 1 at a time, then stir in the rum. Allow to cool.

With an electric mixer, beat the egg whites and cream of tartar until stiff peaks form; do not overbeat. Stir in 1 spoonful of egg whites into the chocolate mixture to lighten, then fold in the remaining egg whites.

Using a ladle or tablespoon, carefully spoon an equal amount of mousse into each of 6 sundae, parfait or wine glasses. Do not touch the edge of the glasses; if any of the mixture drips, wipe the glass clean. Place the glasses on a tray or baking sheet and refrigerate for 1 hour, or until set.

Prepare the milk chocolate mousse as above, then spoon equal amounts over the bittersweet chocolate mousse. Refrigerate for about 1 hour, or until set.

Prepare the white chocolate mousse as above, then spoon equal amounts over the milk chocolate mousse. Cover each glass with plasticwrap and refrigerate for 4–6 hours or overnight, until set.

To serve, spoon 15 ml/1 tbsp chocolate sauce over each mousse. Spoon whipped cream into a small piping bag fitted with a medium star nozzle and pipe a rosette of cream on to each mousse. Decorate with chocolate coffee beans.

Ingredients

Bittersweet chocolate mousse

100 g/4 oz bittersweet chocolate, chopped
¼ cup/60 ml/2 floz whipping cream
15 g/½ oz pieces unsalted butter
2 eggs, separated
1 Tbsp rum
pinch of cream of tartar

Milk chocolate mousse

100 g/4 oz good-quality milk chocolate, chopped
¼ cup/60 ml/2 floz whipping cream
15 g/½ oz pieces unsalted butter
2 eggs, separated
1 Tbsp coffee-flavor liqueur
pinch of cream of tartar

White chocolate mousse

100 g/4 oz good-quality white chocolate, chopped
¼ cup/60 ml/2 floz whipped cream
15 g/½ oz pieces unsalted butter
2 eggs, separated
1 Tbsp coffee-flavor liqueur
pinch of cream of tartar

CHOCOLATE TRIFLE

SERVES 6

Cut the Swiss roll into ½ inch/1 cm slices and arrange over the base and sides of a trifle dish.

Arrange the drained apricots on top.

Pour the cold Chocolate Custard over the apricots.

Pipe the whipped heavy cream over the top. Decorate with chocolate hearts, ratafia cookies, candied cherries etc, as desired.

INGREDIENTS

200 g/7 oz chocolate Swiss roll
420 g/14 oz can apricot halves, drained
2½ cups/600 ml/1 pt Chocolate Custard (see pages 12/13)
1¼ cups/300 ml/½ pt heavy cream, whipped

To decorate

chocolate hearts (see page 165)
ratafia biscuits
candied cherries, etc

CHOCOLATE ROULADE

SERVES 6–8

Preheat the oven to 180°C /350°F. Melt the chocolate in a bowl over a pan of hot water.

Put the egg yolks into a large bowl. Add the sugar and beat well until pale and fluffy.

Add the hot water to the chocolate and stir until smooth. Whisk into the egg mixture.

Whisk the egg whites until stiff. Lightly fold into the chocolate mixture. Pour into a greased and lined 15½ x 9½ inch/39 x 24 cm Swiss roll tin.

Cook in the oven for 15–20 minutes, until firm.

Remove from the oven. Cover with a sheet of greaseproof paper and a damp tea towel. Leave until completely cold.

To make the filling put all the ingredients into a bowl. Whisk until thick. Chill.

Turn the roulade on to a sheet of greaseproof paper dusted with confectioners sugar. Peel away the lining paper.

Spread the filling over the roulade to within 1 inch /2.5 cm of the edge. Roll up like a Swiss roll, using the greaseproof paper to help.

Place seam-side down on a serving plate and chill for 1 hour before serving.

To serve, dredge the roulade with confectioners sugar. Pipe whipped cream down the center and decorate with candied violets and angelica leaves.

INGREDIENTS

175 g/6 oz plain chocolate
5 eggs, separated
1 cup/175 g/6 oz sugar
3 Tbsp hot water
confectioners sugar, sieved

Filling

1¾ cups/425 ml/¾ pt heavy cream
¼ cup/50 g/2 oz confectioners sugar, sieved
⅛ cup/25 g/1 oz unsweetened cocoa powder
2 tsp instant coffee
½ tsp vanilla extract

To decorate

confectioners sugar
whipped cream
crystallized violets
angelica leaves

Ingredients

2 cups/475 ml/16 floz milk

½ cup/100 g/4 oz sugar

225 g/8 oz plain or bittersweet chocolate, chopped

1 Tbsp vanilla extract

2 Tbsp brandy or liqueur

7 egg yolks

To decorate

whipped cream

chopped pistachios

chocolate leaves (see page 12/13)

Chocolate Pots de Crème

SERVES 8

Preheat the oven to 170°C/325°F.

In a saucepan, bring the milk and sugar to the boil. Add the chocolate all at once, stirring frequently until melted and smooth. Stir in the vanilla extract and brandy or liqueur.

In a bowl, beat the egg yolks lightly. Slowly beat in the chocolate mixture until well blended. Strain the custard into a 3½ pt/2 litre measuring jug or large pitcher.

Place 8 ½ cup/120 ml/4 floz *pots de crème* cups or ramekins into a shallow roasting tin. Pour an equal amount of custard into each cup. Pour enough hot water into the tin to come about halfway up the side of the cups.

Bake for 30–35 minutes, until the custard is just set. Shake the pan slightly; the center of each custard should jiggle. Alternatively, insert a knife into the side of 1 custard; the knife should come out clean. Remove the tin from the oven and transfer the cups from the tin to a heat-proof surface to cool completely.

Place the cooled custards on a baking sheet and cover with plasticwrap. Refrigerate until well chilled. (The custards can be stored for 2 days in the refrigerator.)

To serve, decorate the top of each custard with a dollop or rosette of whipped cream. Sprinkle each with chopped pistachios and a chocolate leaf.

Chapter Five

Hot Desserts

MOUTH-WATERING WARM PUDDINGS AND DESSERTS TO CHEER UP EVEN THE COLDEST OF DAYS

Chocolate Soufflé

SERVES 4

Ingredients

2 Tbsp butter
2 Tbsp plain flour
¾ cup/175 ml/6 floz milk
½ tsp vanilla extract
40 g/1½ oz plain chocolate, chopped or grated
3 eggs, separated
¼ cup/50 g/2 oz sugar

Preheat the oven to 180°C/350°F. Melt the butter in a heavy-bottomed pan.

Mix the flour and continue to cook, stirring continuously, until the butter absorbs the flour.

Gradually add the milk, vanilla and chocolate. Continue to cook, stirring constantly, until the chocolate has melted and the sauce has thickened.

Whisk the egg yolks with the sugar until they are light and frothy.

Pour the egg yolk mixture into the chocolate sauce and stir thoroughly but gently.

Whisk the egg whites until they are stiff but not dry, Gently fold into the chocolate mixture, starting with just one spoonful and gradually adding the remainder.

Grease a 4 cups/1 litre/2 pint soufflé dish and sprinkle the base with sugar.

Pour the mixture into the prepared dish. Make a deep cut around the mixture, approximately 1 inch /2½ cm from the edge.

Bake the soufflé until it is well risen and set. Sprinkle with sifted confectioners sugar and serve immediately.

Variations

For a Caramel Soufflé, omit the chocolate and heat 3 tbsp sugar in a heavy-bottomed pan until the sugar has melted and browned. Stir into the thickened sauce before adding the egg yolk mixture.

For a Vanilla Soufflé, heat the milk with a vanilla pod and leave to stand for 1 hour. Remove the vanilla pod and use the milk to make the sauce as above.

CHOCOLATE AND PINE NUT TART

SERVES 7–8

Prepare the pastry. In a food processor process the flour, sugar, and salt. Add the butter and process for 15-20 seconds, until the mixture resembles coarse crumbs. Add the egg yolks and process just until the dough begins to stick together. Turn the dough onto a lightly floured work surface and knead gently until well blended. Shape the dough into a flat disc and wrap tightly in plastic wrap. Refrigerate for 4-5 hours.

Lightly butter a 9 inch, 1½ inch deep pie plate with a removable base. Roll out the dough into an 11 inch circle, 1/4 inch thick and ease the dough into the plate. Press the overhang down, then cut off the excess dough. Press the edge to form a rim about 1/4 inch higher than the plate. Crimp the edge. Prick the bottom of the dough with a fork. Refrigerate for 1 hour.

Preheat the oven to 400°F. Line the shell with foil or waxed paper and fill with dry beans or rice. Bake for 5 minutes, remove the foil and beans and bake for 5 minutes longer, until set. Cool on a wire rack. Lower the oven temperature to 375°F. Beat the eggs, sugar, orange rind, and orange-flavor liqueur. Blend in the cream.

Sprinkle chopped chocolate and pine nuts over the bottom of the shell. Pour the egg-and-cream mixture into the shell and bake for 30-35 minutes, until set. Cool for 10 minutes.

Prepare the glaze. Remove thin strips of orange rind and cut into julienne strips. Over high heat, bring the orange strips, water and sugar to the boil for 5-8 minutes, until the syrup is thickened. Stir in the cold water.

Glaze the tart with sugar syrup and arrange the orange strips over the top. Remove the side of the pie plate and slide the tart onto a plate. Serve warm.

INGREDIENTS

Sweet French tart pastry

1½ cups/225g/8oz all-purpose flour
¼ cup/50g/2 oz fine granulated sugar
¼ tsp salt
100g/4 oz butter, cut into small pieces
3 egg yolks, lightly beaten
1-2 tbsp ice water

Filling

2 eggs
⅓ cup/75g/4 oz of sugar
rind of 1 orange, grated
1 tbsp orange-flavor liqueur
1 cup/250ml/8 floz of whipping cream
100g/4 oz semisweet chocolate, chopped
½ cup/75g/3 oz pine nuts, toasted

Glaze

1 orange
¼ cup/50g/2 oz water
¼ cup/50g/2 oz sugar
1 tbsp cold water

PYREX

CINNAMON CHOCOLATE PAIN PERDU

SERVES 4–6

INGREDIENTS

75–100 g/3–4 oz butter
12–14 slices French bread
175 g/6 oz plain chocolate
2½ cups/600 ml/1 pt milk
2 eggs
2 egg yolks
1 tsp ground cinnamon
¼ cup/50 g/2 oz sugar
confectioners sugar

Preheat the oven to 190°C/375°F. Butter the slices of bread on both sides. Place on a baking tray and bake in the oven for about 5 minutes or until lightly golden. Turn over and bake on the other side until golden, about 2–5 minutes.

Melt the chocolate.

Bring the milk almost to boiling point. Remove from the heat and whisk into the chocolate.

Beat together the eggs, egg yolks, cinnamon and sugar. Pour on the chocolate milk and whisk well.

Arrange the French bread in a large shallow baking dish. Strain the chocolate custard over the bread.

Put the dish into a roasting tin and pour in boiling water to come halfway up the side of the baking dish.

Cook in the oven for 30–40 minutes until lightly set.

Dredge with confectioners sugar and serve with light cream.

Apricot-Glazed White Chocolate Rice Pudding with Bitter Chocolate Sauce

SERVES 10

In a bowl, combine the white raisins, hot water and apricot brandy. Leave to stand for at least 2 hours.

In a heavy-based saucepan, combine the rice, 1 cup/250 ml/8 floz milk, water, butter and ¼ cup/50 g/2 oz sugar. Bring to the boil, stirring occasionally. Reduce the heat, cover and simmer for 18–20 minutes, just until liquid is absorbed.

Meanwhile, preheat the oven to 150°C/ 300°F. Butter a 6¼-8 cups/1.5–2 litre/2½–3½ pt shallow baking dish or soufflé dish and set aside. In a saucepan over a low heat, melt the chocolate with the remaining milk, stirring frequently until smooth. Remove from the heat. In a large bowl, lightly beat the eggs, remaining sugar, cream, vanilla extract, cinnamon and nutmeg. Slowly beat in the melted chocolate until well blended. Stir in the white raisins and any liquid. Stir the egg mixture into the cooked rice mixture until well blended, then pour into the baking dish. Cover with foil.

Set the baking dish into a roasting tin. Fill the tin with hot water to about halfway up the side of the dish. Bake for 30 minutes, uncover and bake for 15–20 minutes longer, until a knife inserted 2 inches/5 cm from the edge of the dish comes out clean; the center should remain slightly moist. Run a sharp knife around the edge of the dish to loosen the pudding from the edge and prevent the center from splitting. Leave to cool for 1 hour.

Meanwhile, prepare the glaze. In a saucepan over medium heat, melt the apricot jelly with the orange juice and apricot brandy or liqueur, stirring until smooth. Gently spoon over the top of the pudding to glaze.

Prepare the chocolate sauce. In a saucepan over low heat, bring the cream and apricot jelly to a boil. Remove from the heat and stir in the chocolate, stirring until melted and smooth. Press through a sieve and stir in the apricot brandy or liqueur; keep warm. Serve with the glazed rice pudding.

Ingredients

100 g/4 oz white raisins
3 Tbsp hot water
2 Tbsp apricot brandy or orange-flavor liqueur
1 cup/150 g/5 oz medium- or long-grain white rice
1½ cups/350 ml/12 floz milk
1 cup/250 ml/8 floz water
25g/1 oz butter
½ cup/100 g/4 oz sugar
175 g/6 oz good-quality white chocolate, chopped
3 eggs
2 cups/475 ml/16 floz heavy cream
2 tsp vanilla extract
1 tsp ground cinnamon
½ tsp grated nutmeg

Apricot glaze

½ cup/120 ml/4 floz apricot jelly
1 Tbsp orange juice or water
1 Tbsp apricot brandy or orange-flavor liqueur

Bitter chocolate sauce

¾ cup/175 ml/6 floz heavy cream
¾ cup/175 ml/6 floz apricot jelly
175 g/6 floz bittersweet chocolate, chopped
2 Tbsp apricot brandy or orange-flavor liqueur

CHOCOLATE CRÊPES
WITH PINEAPPLE AND BITTER CHOCOLATE SAUCE

MAKES 12

INGREDIENTS

⅓ cup/45 g/1¾ oz plain flour
1 Tbsp cocoa powder
1 tsp sugar
¼ tsp salt
2 eggs
¾ cup/175 ml/6 floz milk
25 g/1 oz unsalted butter, melted plus extra for reheating crêpes
1 tsp vanilla extract
vegetable oil for greasing

Pineapple filling

25 g/1 oz unsalted butter
1 pineapple, peeled, cored and cut into ½ inch/1 cm pieces or 450 g/1 lb can pineapple pieces in juice, drained
½ tsp ground cinnamon
¼ cup/60 ml/2 floz natural maple syrup
50 g/2 oz plain or milk chocolate chips
50 g/2 oz macadamia nuts, chopped and toasted

Chocolate sauce

100 g/4 oz plain chocolate, chopped
⅓ cup/75 ml/2½ floz water
2 Tbsp natural maple syrup
25 g/1 oz unsalted butter, cut into pieces
confectioners sugar for dusting
fresh cranberries or raspberries and mint leaves for decoration

Into a bowl, sift the flour, cocoa powder, sugar and salt. Mix to blend; make a well in the center.

In another bowl, lightly beat the eggs with the milk. Gradually add to the well in the center of the flour mixture. Using a whisk, blend in the flour from the sides of the bowl to form a paste, then a batter; beat until smooth. Stir in the melted butter and vanilla extract and strain into another bowl. Leave to stand for 1 hour.

With a pastry brush, brush the bottom of a 7 or 8 inch/17.5 or 20 cm crêpe pan with a little vegetable oil. Heat the pan over a medium heat. Stir the batter (if the batter is too thick, stir in a little milk or water; it should be thin.) Fill a ¼ cup/60 ml/2 floz measure or small ladle three-quarters full with batter, then pour into the hot pan. Quickly tilt and rotate pan to cover the bottom of the pan with a thin layer of batter. Cook over a medium-high heat for 1–2 minutes, until the top is set and the bottom is golden. With a palette knife, loosen the edge of the crêpe from the pan, turn over and cook for 30–45 seconds, just until set. Turn out on to a plate.

Continue making crêpes, stirring the batter occasionally and brushing the pan lightly with oil. (A non-stick pan is ideal and does not need additional greasing.) Stack crêpes with sheets of greaseproof paper between each. Set aside.

Prepare the filling. In a large frying pan over medium-high heat, melt the butter until sizzling. Add the pineapple pieces and sauté until golden, 3–4 minutes. Sprinkle with cinnamon and stir in the maple syrup. Cook for 1–2 minutes longer, until the pineapple is lightly coated with syrup and the liquid has evaporated. Remove from the heat.

Lay a crêpe on a plate or work surface, bottom side down. Spoon a little pineapple mixture on to the top half of the crêpe. Sprinkle over a few chocolate chips and macadamia nuts. Fold the bottom half over, then fold into quarters. Continue using all the crêpes, pineapple filling, chocolate chips and nuts. Set each one on a buttered baking sheet and cover tightly with foil until ready to serve.

Prepare the chocolate sauce. In a medium saucepan over a low heat, melt the chocolate with water and maple syrup, stirring frequently until smooth and well blended. Stir in the butter. Keep warm.

Preheat the oven to 190°C/375°F. Uncover the crêpes, brush the top of each with melted butter and re-cover tightly. Bake for 5 minutes just until heated through. Place on a dessert plate or individual plates. Dust with confectioners sugar and decorate with fresh cranberries or raspberries and mint leaves. Serve the chocolate sauce separately.

Magic Chocolate Dessert

SERVES 4 TO 5

The magic in this pudding refers to the delicious sauce that forms at the base of the dessert while it is cooking.

Pre-heat the oven to 175°C/350°F.

To make the sponge, put the dry ingredients into a bowl. Add the butter, milk and a few drops of vanilla extract and mix to form a thick batter.

Pour the mixture into a well-buttered 18 cm/17 in ovenproof dish.

To make the sauce, mix together the brown sugar, cocoa powder and boiling water. Pour this sauce over the batter.

Bake in the oven for about 40 minutes. During cooking the chocolate sponge rises to the top, and a chocolate fudge sauce forms underneath. Serve with vanilla ice cream.

Ingredients

150 g/5 oz self-raising flour, sifted
¼ cup/50 g/2 oz sugar
2 Tbsp unsweetened cocoa powder, sifted
50 g/2 oz walnuts or pecans, chopped
50 g/2 oz butter, melted
¾ cup/150 ml/5 fl oz milk
Vanilla extract

Sauce

½ cup/100 g/4 oz soft brown sugar
2 Tbsp unsweetened cocoa powder, sifted
200 ml/7 fl oz boiling water
Vanilla ice cream to serve

Baked Alaska

SERVES 6–8

Ingredients

3¾ pt cups/900 ml/1½ pt chocolate ice cream
3 eggs
⅓ cup/75 g/3 oz sugar
½ cup/65 g/2½ oz plain flour
2 Tbsp unsweetened cocoa powder
approximately 225 g/8 oz fruit (strawberries, bananas, raspberries or cherries)
4 Tbsp Marsala or sweet sherry
4 egg whites
1 cup/225 g/8 oz sugar

Pack the ice cream into a 1 lb/450 g loaf tin lined with greaseproof paper. Freeze overnight.

Preheat the oven to 200°C/400°F. Put the eggs and sugar into a bowl and whisk until thick and creamy, and the whisk leaves a trail.

Sieve the flour and cocoa and fold gently into the mixture.

Turn into a greased and lined 9 inch/ 23 cm tin. Bake in the oven for 12–15 minutes. Cool and remove the lining.

Prepare the fruit by slicing it and removing stones if necessary. Put into a bowl with the Marsala or sherry.

Whisk the egg whites until stiff. Whisk in the sugar a little at a time. Spoon the meringue into a piping bag fitted with a large star nozzle.

Trim the edges of the sponge, then cut 2.5 cm/1 inch strips from 2 sides of the cake to make an oblong slightly larger than the ice cream block.

Preheat the oven to 230°C/450°F. Put the sponge on an ovenproof serving dish. Spoon the fruit and juices over the sponge.

Remove the ice cream from the freezer and turn it on to the sponge. Remove the paper.

Quickly pipe the meringue decoratively over the ice cream, covering it completely.

Bake in the oven for 3–5 minutes until lightly browned. Cut into slices and serve immediately.

Chapter Six

Sweets and Treats

DELICIOUS AND FUN,
THESE CHOCOLATE FANCIES
ARE IDEAL FOR SPECIAL
OCCASIONS

Chocolate-Coated Toffee

MAKES ABOUT 750 G (1½ LB)

Ingredients

150 g/5 oz pecans (optional)
225 g/8 oz unsalted butter, cut into pieces
3½ cups/350 g/12 oz sugar
¼ tsp cream of tartar
175 g/6 oz plain chocolate, finely chopped

Preheat the oven to 180°C/350°F. Place the pecans (if using) on a small baking sheet and bake for 10–12 minutes, until well toasted. Leave to cool completely, then chop and set aside.

Line a 9 inch/23 cm square cake tin with foil. Invert the tin and mold the foil over the bottom. Turn the tin right side up and line with the molded foil. Generously butter the bottom and sides of the foil.

In a heavy-based saucepan over a medium heat, melt the butter. Stir in the sugar and cream of tartar, stirring until the sugar dissolves. Bring the mixture to the boil. Cover the pan for 2 minutes so steam washes down any sugar crystals which collect on the side of the pan. Uncover and continue cooking for 10–12 minutes, or until the toffee reaches 154°C/310°F on a sweet thermometer.

Carefully pour into the tin and leave to rest for about 1 minute. Sprinkle the top of the toffee with chocolate and leave for 2 minutes until the chocolate softens. Using the back of a spoon or a wide-bladed knife, spread the chocolate evenly over the toffee until smooth. Sprinkle evenly with the chopped pecans (if using). Cool to room temperature, then refrigerate until firm and cold.

Using the foil as a guide, remove the toffee from the tin. With the back of a heavy knife or hammer, break the toffee into large, irregular pieces.

Merry
Christmas

Icy Christmas Puddings

MAKES 30

Ingredients

⅔ cup/150 ml/¼ pt milk
40 g/1½ oz plain chocolate, finely chopped
2 egg yolks, size 5–6
¼ cup/40 g/1½ oz caster sugar
75 g/3 oz praline, finely crushed (purchased)
⅔ cup/150 ml/¼ pt heavy cream, whipped

To coat

275 g/10 oz plain chocolate, melted and cooled

To decorate

100 g/4 oz marzipan (purchsed)
food colorings

Place the milk and chocolate in a small saucepan, and heat gently to melt the chocolate and warm the milk.

Beat together the egg yolks and sugar, and beat in the chocolate milk.

Strain the custard back into the saucepan, and heat very gently, stirring until slightly thickened. Add the praline.

Pour the hot custard into a freezer-proof container, cool, and then freeze for 2–3 hours until slushy.

Beat the ice-cream thoroughly and fold in the cream.

Freeze for a further 2 hours, and beat again. Leave to freeze completely.

Meanwhile, roll out the marzipan thinly, and cut out 30 small shapes to top the puddings. Color the remaining scraps of marzipan to make holly leaves and berries.

When the ice-cream has frozen, scoop out small balls with a melon baller, quickly coat with chocolate, and top with the marzipan 'cream', leaves and berries. Return to the freezer until required.

CHOCOLATE TURTLES

MAKES ABOUT 30

Oil 2 baking sheets with the vegetable oil. Prepare the caramel coating.

When the caramel has cooled for a few minutes, stir in the nuts until they are coated. Do not overwork or the caramel will crystallize. Using an oiled tablespoon, drop spoonfuls of caramel-nut mixture on to the prepared baking sheet, about 1 inch/2.5 cm apart. If the caramel-nut mixtures becomes too hard, reheat over low heat for several minutes until softened. Refrigerate until firm and cold.

Using a palette knife, transfer the nut clusters to a wire rack over a baking sheet to catch the drips. In a saucepan over a low heat, melt the chocolate and vegetable fat, stirring occasionally until smooth; cool the chocolate to about 30°C (88°F).

Using a tablespoon, spoon the chocolate over the nut clusters, being sure to coat completely, spreading the chocolate over the surface. Return the drips to the saucepan and reheat gently to completely cover all the clusters. Leave to set for about 2 hours at room temperature. Store in a cool place in an airtight container with foil between the layers, but do not refrigerate.

INGREDIENTS

vegetable oil
Caramel Coating (see page 163)
275 g/10 oz hazelnuts, pecans, walnuts or unsalted peanuts or a combination
350 g/12 oz plain chocolate, chopped
2 Tbsp white vegetable fat

WHITE CHOCOLATE FUDGE LAYER

MAKES 36 TRIANGLES

INGREDIENTS

- 600 g/1¼ lb good-quality white chocolate, chopped
- 400 g/14 oz can sweetened condensed milk
- 2 tsp vanilla extract
- 1½ tsp white vinegar or lemon juice
- pinch of salt
- 250 g/9 oz unsalted macadamia nuts
- 175 g/6 oz plain chocolate, chopped
- 40 g/1½ oz unsalted butter, cut into pieces
- 25 g/1 oz plain chocolate, melted, for piping

Line a 8 inch/20 cm square cake tin with foil. Invert the tin. Mold the foil over the bottom, then turn the cake tin right side up and line with the foil. Grease the bottom and sides of the foil. Set aside.

In a saucepan over a low heat, melt the chocolate with the condensed milk, stirring frequently until smooth. Remove from the heat and stir in the vanilla extract, vinegar and salt until well blended. Stir in the nuts. Spread half of the white chocolate mixture in the tin. Refrigerate for 15 minutes or until firm; keep the remaining mixture warm.

In a saucepan over a low heat, melt the chopped chocolate and butter, stirring frequently until smooth. Cool slightly; pour over the white chocolate layer and refrigerate until firm, about 15 minutes.

If necessary, gently reheat the remaining white chocolate mixture then pour over the set chocolate layer, smoothing the top evenly. Refrigerate for 2–4 hours, until completely firm.

Using the foil as a guide, remove the set fudge from the tin. With a knife, cut into 16 squares. Cut each square diagonally in half, making 36 triangles. Place the fudge triangles on to a wire rack placed over a baking sheet to catch the drips.

Spoon the melted chocolate into a small paper cone and drizzle chocolate over the fudge triangles. Store in an airtight container in the refrigerator for 1–2 weeks.

CHOCOLATE EGGS

MAKES 4

INGREDIENTS

4 medium eggs
225 g/8 oz plain or milk chocolate
75 g/3 oz praline, ground finely
2 Tbsp cream

Using an egg prick or pin, pierce a hole at the pointed end of each egg.

Using small scissors, carefully enlarge the hole to about ½ inch/1 cm.

Push a cocktail stick or toothpick into the hole to puncture the yolk. Shake the raw egg into a bowl.

Run water gently into the shells and shake until they are clean. Turn upside down and leave to dry.

Melt the chocolate. Stir in the praline and cream. Spoon or pour the chocolate into the dry shells. Leave until set.

Seal the holes with small round labels and place the eggs in an egg box, holed side down.

MERINGUE MUSHROOMS

MAKES ABOUT 8

INGREDIENTS

1 egg white
¼ cup/50 g/2 oz caster sugar
50 g/2 oz plain chocolate, melted
cocoa powder, to serve

Preheat the oven to 140°C/275°F. Whisk the egg white until stiff.

Whisk in the sugar a little at a time until the mixture is stiff and glossy.

Put the meringue into a piping bag fitted with a ½ inch/1 cm plain nozzle.

Line a baking sheet with greaseproof paper. Pipe 6–8 small mounds of meringue about 1 inch/2.5 cm in diameter to form the mushrooms caps.

Next pipe 6–8 smaller mounds, drawing each one up to a point, to represent the stalks.

Bake in the oven for about 1 hour until dry and crisp. Allow to cool.

Using the point of a sharp knife, make a tiny hole in the base of each mushroom cap.

Spread a little melted chocolate on the underside of each cap and gently push on a stalk. Allow to set.

Before serving, dust the mushrooms with a little cocoa powder.

BOW TIES

MAKES 14

INGREDIENTS

50 g/2 oz plain chocolate, chopped
15 g/½ oz unsalted butter
1 x 5 ml sp/1 tsp golden syrup
15 g/½ oz Puffed Rice, finely crushed
225 g/8 oz marzipan (purchased)
food colorings
confectioners sugar for rolling out
14 sugar flowers

Place the chocolate, butter and syrup in a small saucepan, and heat very gently until melted.

Remove pan from heat and thoroughly mix in Puffed Rice.

Turn mixture into a bowl, and refrigerate until firm enough to handle.

Meanwhile, divide up the marzipan, add a few drops of colouring to each portion, and gently knead in, making as many different colors as you wish.

Sprinkle the surface with confectioners sugar, and roll out one colour at a time, about ¼ inch/0.6 cm thick.

Cut out bow ties about 2 inch /5 cm thick.

Mould the Puffed Rice mixture into small balls, shape around the center of each bow tie, and top with sugar flowers.

Leave for several hours until firm.

EASY CHOCOLATE TRUFFLES

MAKES ABOUT 45

INGREDIENTS

⅝ cup/150 ml/5 floz whipping cream
250 g/9 oz plain chocolate, chopped
30 ml/2 Tbsp brandy or other liqueur (optional)
⅓ cup/50 g/2 oz cocoa powder

In a saucepan over a low heat, bring the cream to the boil. Remove the pan from the heat. Add the chocolate all at once, stirring frequently until smooth. Stir in the liqueur if using. Strain into a bowl and cool to room temperature. Refrigerate for 1 hour, until thickened and firm.

Line 2 small baking sheets with foil. Using a melon baller, a 1 inch/2.5 cm ice-cream scoop or a teaspoon, form the mixture into 1 inch /2.5 cm balls and place on the baking sheets. Refrigerate for 1–2 hours, until the balls are firm.

Place the cocoa powder in a small bowl. Drop each chocolate ball into the cocoa and turn with your fingers to coat with cocoa. Roll the balls between the palms of your hands, dusting with more cocoa if necessary. Do not try to make them perfectly round; they should look slightly irregular. Place on the baking sheets. Add more cocoa to the bowl if necessary.

Shake the cocoa-coated truffles in a dry sieve to remove excess cocoa, then store, covered, in the refrigerator for up to 2 weeks or freeze for up to 2 months. Soften for 10 minutes at room temperature before serving.

CHOCOLATE-DIPPED CARAMEL APPLES

MAKES 12

INGREDIENTS

vegetable oil
12 small apples, well scrubbed and dried
90 g/3½ oz pecans, walnuts or hazelnuts, finely chopped and toasted (optional)
175 g/6 oz chocolate, chopped

Caramel coating

2 cups/520 ml/18 floz heavy cream
1½ cups/350 ml/12 floz golden syrup
40 g/1½ oz unsalted butter, cut into pieces
1¼ cups/225 g/8 oz granulated sugar
½ cup/90 g/3½ oz brown sugar
pinch of salt
15 ml/1 Tbsp vanilla extract

Oil a baking sheet with the vegetable oil. Insert a wooden lollipop stick firmly into the stem end of each apple; do not use metal sticks or small pointed wooden skewers as they could be harmful to children.

Prepare the caramel coating. In a heavy-based saucepan, stir the cream, syrup, butter, sugars and salt. Cook over medium heat, stirring occasionally, until the sugars dissolve and the butter is melted, about 3 minutes. Bring the mixture to the boil and cook, stirring frequently, until the caramel mixture reaches 116°C/240°F (soft ball stage) on a sugar thermometer, about 20 minutes. Place the bottom of the saucepan in a pan of cold water to stop cooking or transfer to a small, cold saucepan. Cool to about 104°C/220°F; this will take 10–15 minutes. Stir in the vanilla extract.

Holding each apple by the wooden stick, quickly dip each apple into the hot caramel, turning to coat on all sides and covering the apple completely. Scrape the bottom of the apple against the edge of the saucepan to remove the excess; place on the prepared baking sheet. If necessary, reheat the caramel slightly to thin it. Leave the apples to cool for 15–20 minutes, until the caramel hardens.

If using, place the nuts in a bowl. In the top of a double boiler over a low heat, melt the chocolate, stirring frequently until smooth. Remove from the heat. Dip each caramel-coated apple about two-thirds of the way into the chocolate, allowing the excess to drip off, then drip into the nuts. Place on a greaseproof paper-lined baking sheet. Leave to set for 1 hour, until the chocolate hardens.

TROPICAL DELIGHTS

MAKES 25

INGREDIENTS

175 g/6 oz clear honey
150 g/5 oz golden syrup
75 g/3 oz unsalted butter, diced
100 g/4 oz Tropical dried fruit mix, roughly chopped
100 g/4 oz plain chocolate or carob, chopped

To decorate

a little extra Tropical mix

Place the honey, syrup and butter in a saucepan, and heat gently, stirring occasionally until the butter has melted.

Bring to the boil, and boil steadily to the hard ball stage, 130°C/250°F.

Remove immediately from the heat, stir in the Tropical mix, and pour into an oiled, shallow, 7 inch/18 cm square tin.

Place the chocolate or carob in a small bowl over a pan of hot water, and stir occasionally until melted.

Pour the chocolate into the tin to cover the Tropical Delights, and decorate with Tropical mix.

Mark into squares when starting to set, and leave to set completely.

St. Valentine's Casket

MAKES 1 CASKET

Place the sugar and water in a saucepan, and heat gently, stirring occasionally, until the sugar has dissolved.

Bring to the boil, without stirring, until light golden in color.

Add the peppermint extract, and pour the syrup onto a lightly oiled baking sheet. Leave to set, then crush finely.

Place the milk chocolate in a small bowl over a pan of hot water, and stir occasionally until melted.

Remove bowl from pan, stir in the crushed mint caramel, and spread into a 10 inch/25 cm square on waxed paper. Leave to set.

Meanwhile, make the casket. Melt the plain chocolate as in step 4, cool slightly, and spread into a 8 inch/20 cm square on waxed paper. Leave to set.

Cut out 2 hexagonals approximately 4 inches/10 cm from point to point, and 6 sides for the casket. Melt the scraps of chocolate, and brush a little onto the edges of the base and sides, to assemble.

Using a cutter, cut out heart shapes from the chocolate mint squares. Melt the scraps for extra hearts if wished.

Fill the casket with hearts and flowers, attach the lid, and decorate with ribbons.

Ingredients

Hearts

½ cup/100 g/4 oz caster sugar

125 ml/4 floz water

½ cup x 5 ml sp/½ tsp peppermint extract

225 g/8 oz milk chocolate, chopped

Casket

75 g/3 oz plain chocolate, chopped

To decorate

flowers and ribbons

CHOCOLATE-MINT CRISPS

MAKES ABOUT 30

INGREDIENTS

vegetable oil for greasing
4 Tbsp sugar
¼ cup/60 ml/2 floz water
5 ml/1 tsp peppermint extract
225 g/8 oz plain chocolate, chopped

Grease a baking sheet with vegetable oil. Set aside. In a saucepan, bring the sugar and water to the boil, swirling the pan until the sugar dissolves. Boil rapidly until the sugar reaches 140°C/280°F on a sugar thermometer. Remove the pan from the heat and stir in the peppermint extract. Pour on to the greased baking sheet and allow to set; do not touch as the sugar syrup is very hot and can cause serious burns.

When the mixture is cold, use a rolling pin to break it up into pieces. Place the pieces into a food processor fitted with the metal blade and process until fine crumbs form; do not overprocess.

Line 2 baking sheets with greaseproof paper or foil; grease the paper or foil. In the top of a double boiler over a low heat, melt the chocolate, stirring frequently until smooth. Remove from the heat and stir in the ground mint mixture.

Using a teaspoon, drop small mounds of mixture on to the prepared baking sheets. Using the back of the spoon, spread into 1 inch/2.5 cm circles. Cool, then refrigerate to set, at least 1 hour. Peel off the paper or foil and store in airtight containers with greaseproof paper between each layer. Store in the refrigerator for 1 week.

EASTER EGG

MAKES 1

INGREDIENTS

200 g/7 oz chocolate for 1 × 7 in high/18 cm egg
225 g/8 oz chocolate for 2–3 × 4 in/10 cm eggs
450 g/1 lb chocolate for 1 × 8 in/20 cm egg

Chop the chocolate and place in a small bowl over a pan of hot water. Stir occasionally until melted.

Remove the bowl from the pan, and spoon a little of the chocolate into a clean and dry Easter egg mold.

Tilt the mold until it is evenly coated, and pour any excess chocolate back into the bowl.

Place the mold upside down on waxed paper, and leave to set. Add another 1–2 coats of chocolate in the same way if using large molds.

Cut off any excess chocolate from the edge of the mold, and ease the egg out.

Paint the edge of one half of each egg with a little melted chocolate, and gently press the two halves together, holding with greaseproof paper. Leave to set.

Chocolate-Dipped Fruit

MAKES ABOUT 12

Clean and prepare the fruit. Wipe the strawberries with a soft cloth or brush gently with a pastry brush; wash and dry firm-skinned fruits such as cherries and grapes. Dry well and set on paper towels to absorb any remaining moisture. Peel or cut any other fruits being used. Dried or candied fruits can also be used.

In the top of a double boiler over a low heat, melt the white chocolate, stirring frequently until smooth. Remove from heat and cool to tepid, about 28°C/84°F, stirring frequently.

Line a baking sheet with greaseproof paper or foil. Holding the fruit by the stem or end and at an angle, dip about two-thirds of the fruit into the chocolate. Allow the excess to drip off and place on the baking sheet. Continue dipping the fruit; if the chocolate becomes too thick, set over hot water again briefly to soften slightly. Refrigerate the fruit until the chocolate sets, about 20 minutes.

In the top of the cleaned double boiler over low heat, melt the plain chocolate, stirring frequently until smooth. Remove from the heat and cool to just below body temperature, about 30°C/88°F.

Remove each white chocolate-coated fruit from the baking sheet and holding each by the stem or end, and at the opposite angle, dip the bottom third of each piece into the dark chocolate, creating a chevron effect. Set on the baking sheet. Refrigerate for 5 minutes, or until set. Remove from the refrigerator 10–15 minutes before serving to soften the chocolate.

Ingredients

about 12 pieces of fruit, such as strawberries; cherries; orange segments; kiwi fruit; fresh peeled lychees; Cape gooseberries; stoned prunes; stoned dates; dried apricots; dried pears; nuts

175 g/6 oz good-quality white chocolate, chopped

75 g/3 oz plain chocolate, chopped

HONEYCOMB CHUNKS

MAKES 36 PIECES

INGREDIENTS

1½ cups/450 g/1 lb light muscavado sugar
1¼ cups/300 ml/½ pt water
4 x 156 ml sp/4 Tbsp vinegar
3 x 3 Tbsp golden syrup
1½ tsp cinnamon
½ tsp smoothed bicarbonate of soda
225 g/8 oz carob, chopped

Place the sugar, water, vinegar and syrup in a saucepan, and heat gently, stirring occasionally, until the sugar has dissolved completely.

Bring to the boil, without stirring, and boil steadily to the soft crack stage, 141°C /285°F on a sugar thermometer.

Remove immediately from the heat, stir in the cinnamon and bicarbonate of soda, and allow the bubbles to subside a little before pouring into a 8 inch/20 cm lightly oiled square tin.

Leave to set slightly, mark into squares, and allow to set completely.

Place the carob in a small bowl over a pan of hot water, and stir occasionally until melted. Remove bowl from pan.

Break up the honeycomb and dip the pieces in the carob to coat. Leave to set.

Ginger Bells

MAKES 18 DEPENDING ON MOLD SIZE

Melt the chocolate and use to make bells in chocolate moulds. Use plastic moulds for unusual shapes like bells (purchased). Spoon in some melted chocolate, and tip mould to coat it evenly. Pour off the excess and dry upside down on non-stick paper. Tap gently to remove from mould. Fill chocolates with centres before removing from their moulds for best results.)

Mix together the sugar, glucose powder and gelatin in a small saucepan, stir in the apple juice and ginger syrup, and heat gently to dissolve. Leave to cool.

Divide the stem ginger between the bells, pour in the apple and ginger jelly, and leave to set until firm.

Fix the bell halves together to finish or seal the jelly in with melted chocolate. Eat within a few days.

Ingredients

175 g/6 oz chocolate, chopped – use plain, white or milk for variety

½ cup/75 g/3 oz caster sugar

⅛ cup/25 g/1 oz glucose powder

15 g/½ oz gelatine

¼ cup/65 ml/2½ floz apple juice

1 Tbsp stem ginger syrup

25 g/1 oz stem ginger, finely chopped

CHOCOLATE-STUFFED FIGS AND PRUNES

MAKES 24

INGREDIENTS

12 large fresh figs
12 extra-large stoned prunes, preferably presoaked or softened
40 g/1½ oz unsalted butter, softened
75 g/3 oz blanched almonds, chopped and toasted
1 egg yolk
1 tsp Amaretto liqueur
75 g/3 oz plain chocolate, melted and cooled

Chocolate for dipping

225 g/8 oz plain chocolate, chopped
65 g/2½ oz unsalted butter, cut into pieces

In a food processor fitted with the metal blade, process the butter, almonds, egg yolk and liqueur until creamy. With the machine running, slowly pour in the melted chocolate and process until well blended. Scrape into a bowl and refrigerate for about 1 hour, until firm enough to pipe.

Line a baking sheet with greaseproof paper. Pipe the mixture into the figs and prunes. Place the filled fruits on the baking sheet and chill for 30 minutes.

In a saucepan over a low heat, melt the chocolate and butter, stirring frequently until melted and smooth. Leave to cool to room temperature, about 30 minutes, stirring occasionally.

Insert a toothpick into each filled fruit. Dip each into the melted chocolate and allow the excess to drip off. Using another toothpick, push the fruit off the inserted toothpick on to the lined baking sheet. Alternatively, dip the filled fruits about two-thirds of the way into the chocolate, leaving one-third exposed. Place on the baking sheet. Refrigerate for at least 1 hour to set.

Using a thin-bladed knife, remove the fruit from the baking sheet to paper cases. Remove from the refrigerator about 30 minutes before serving.

Chocolate Caramel Popcorn

SERVES 3–4

Ingredients

¼ cup/50 g/2 oz brown sugar
25 g/1 oz butter
1½ Tbsp golden syrup
1 tbsp milk
50 g/2 oz chocolate chips
a pinch of bicarbonate of soda
5 cups/1.1 litres/2 pt popped popcorn

Preheat the oven to 150°C/300°F. Put the sugar, butter, syrup and milk into a heavy-based saucepan.

Stir over a gentle heat until the butter and sugar have melted. Bring to the boil.

Boil without stirring for 2 minutes.

Remove from the heat. Add the chocolate and bicarbonate of soda. Stir until the chocolate is melted.

Measure the popped popcorn into a bowl. Pour over the syrup and toss well until evenly coated.

Spread the mixture on a large baking sheet. Bake in the oven for about 15 minutes. Test for crispness. Bake for a further 5–10 minutes if necessary. Cool.

ROCKY ROAD LOLLIPOPS

MAKES 10

INGREDIENTS

100 g/4 oz milk chocolate, chopped
50 g/2 oz unsalted butter, diced
4 marshmallows
4 candied cherries
15 g/½ oz unsalted peanuts
⅓ cup/75 g/3 oz confectioners sugar, sifted
25 g/1 oz sugar strands
10 lolly sticks

Place the chocolate and butter in a small saucepan, and heat very gently until melted. Turn into a bowl.

Chop the marshmallows, cherries and peanuts very finely, and stir into the chocolate and butter with the confectioners sugar.

Leave until firm enough to handle if necessary, then shape into 10 balls.

Roll balls in sugar strands, and press onto sticks.

PEANUT BUTTER CORNETS

MAKES 8

INGREDIENTS

8 sugar ice-cream cones
100 g/4 oz milk chocolate, chopped
4 tbsp crunchy peanut butter
15 g/½ oz unsalted peanuts, finely chopped and toasted

Slice about 1 inch/2.5 cm off the top of each cone, and crush well.

Place the chocolate and peanut butter in a small saucepan, and heat very gently until melted. Stir in the crushed cone tops.

Pour or spoon the mixture into the cones, sprinkle with the chopped peanuts, and leave to set.

Prune and Two Chocolate Pieces

MAKES 25

These delectable pieces can be served with after dinner coffee or arranged in an attractive box as a gift. Choose the ready to eat type of prune to avoid having to soak them.

Preheat oven to 190°C/375°F. Grease and base-line an 20 x 20 cm/8 x 8 inch pan.

Chop the prunes and place in a saucepan with the sherry or orange juice and water. Bring to a boil and cook for 2 minutes, stirring all the time. Leave to cool.

Mix the flour, cinnamon, and oats, blend in the butter and stir in the sugar.

Stir in the white chocolate chips, lastly the prune mixture. Press into the pan and bake for 12 to 15 minutes or until just starting to turn golden. Leave in the pan to cool.

Melt the remaining chocolate and pour over the bake. Using a sharp knife, cut into squares while still warm. Drizzle with more melted white chocolate, if liked. Store in an airtight container.

Ingredients

1 cup prunes
1 Tbsp sweet sherry or orange juice
2 Tbsp water
½ cup/50 g/2 oz self-rising flour
1 tsp powdered cinnamon
1 cup/100 g/4 oz rolled oats
15 g/½ oz lightly salted butter
¼ cup/50 g/2 oz packed soft brown sugar
½ cup/100g /4 oz white chocolate chips
50 g/2 oz milk or semi-sweet chocolate

Ingredients

625 g/22 oz bittersweet chocolate, chopped
75 g/3 oz unsalted butter, cut into pieces
75 ml/2½ floz seedless raspberry jelly
2 tbsp raspberry-flavor liqueur
350 g/12 oz chocolate, chopped

Chocolate-Coated Raspberry Truffles

MAKES ABOUT 24

In a saucepan over low heat, melt 275 g /10 oz chocolate, butter and jelly, stirring frequently until smooth and well blended. Remove from the heat and stir in the liqueur. Strain into a bowl and cool. Refrigerate for 2–3 hours, until firm.

Line a baking sheet with greaseproof paper or foil. Using a melon baller, a 1 inch/2.5 cm ice-cream scoop or a teaspoon, form the mixture into balls. Place on the baking sheet and freeze for 1 hour, or until very firm.

In the top of a double boiler over low heat, melt the remaining chocolate, stirring frequently until smooth; the chocolate should be 46–48°C/115–120°F. Remove from the heat and pour into a clean bowl; cool to about 30°C/88°F.

Using a fork, dip the truffles, 1 at a time, into the chocolate, coating completely and tapping the fork on the edge of the bowl to shake off the excess. Place on the prepared baking sheet. Refrigerate until the chocolate is set, about 1 hour. Store in an airtight container with paper towels covering the truffles to collect any moisture for up to 2 weeks or 1 month in freezer.

COCONUT BONFIRES

MAKES 12

INGREDIENTS

225 g/8 oz milk chocolate, chopped
25 g/1 oz unsalted butter, diced
1½ Tbsp coffee powder
225 g /8 oz coconut ice (recipe on page 12), crushed

To decorate

20 g/¾ oz each of grated white and milk chocolate
12 jelly diamonds

Place the chocolate, butter and coffee powder in a bowl over a pan of hot water, and stir occasionally until melted.

Remove the bowl from the pan, stir in the coconut ice, and leave the mixture to cool and thicken slightly.

Mold or spoon the mixture to cool and thicken slightly.

Mold or spoon the mixture into 12 mounds on waxed paper.

Sprinkle each bonfire with grated chocolate, and top with a jelly diamond.

CHOCOLATE CRUNCH ANIMALS

MAKES 12

INGREDIENTS

100 g/4 oz milk chocolate, chopped
15 g/½ oz unsalted butter
40 g/1½ oz praline, finely crushed (purchased)

To decorate

small sweets

Place the chocolate and butter in a small bowl over a pan of hot water, and stir gently until melted.

Remove bowl from pan, and stir in the crushed praline.

Pour the mixture into a shallow tin, approximately 6 inches/15 cm square and lined with waxed paper, and leave to set.

When set, cut out animal shapes with cutters, melting the scraps and setting again if wished.

Milk Chocolate and Pistachio-Coated Truffles

MAKES ABOUT 24

Ingredients

½ cup/120 ml/4 floz heavy or whipping cream
350 g/12 oz good-quality milk chocolate, chopped
15 g/½ oz unsalted butter
15 ml/1 Tbsp almond- or hazelnut-flavor liqueur
350 g/12 oz bittersweet chocolate, chopped
150 g/5 oz shelled and unsalted pistachio nuts, finely chopped

In a medium saucepan over a medium heat, bring the cream to the boil. Remove from the heat. Add the chocolate all at once, stirring until melted. Stir in the butter and liqueur. Strain into a bowl. Refrigerate for 1 hour or until firm.

Line a baking sheet with greaseproof paper or foil. Using a melon baller, a 1 inch/2.5 cm ice-cream scoop or a teaspoon, form the mixture into balls. Place on a baking sheet and freeze for 1 hour, or until very firm.

In the top of a double boiler over a low heat, melt the bittersweet chocolate, stirring frequently until smooth; the chocolate should be about 46–48°C /115–120°F. Remove from the heat and pour into a clean bowl; cool to about 30°C/88°F.

Place the pistachios in a bowl. Using a fork, dip the truffles, 1 at a time, into the chocolate, coating completely and tapping the fork on the edge of the bowl to shake off the excess. Immediately drop into the bowl of pistachios and roll to coat the chocolate completely. Place on the prepared baking sheet. Refrigerate until set, about 1 hour. Store in an airtight container with paper towels covering the truffles to collect any moisture for up to 2 weeks or 1 month in the freezer.

Highball Cups

MAKES 10

Place the fudge in a small bowl over a pan of hot water, and stir until melted.

Remove the bowl from the pan, and stir in the whisky. Cool slightly.

Divide the stem ginger between the chocolate cups and spoon the fudge into each one. Leave to set.

Pipe a little melted chocolate onto each cup, and decorate with small pieces of chopped stem ginger.

Ingredients

100 g/4 oz fudge (purchased)
2 tsp whisky
2 tsp chopped stem ginger
10 plain chocolate cups (see below)

To decorate

stem ginger

To make chocolate cups

These are made with small foil or paper sweet cases., If using paper use two cases for extra strenght. spoon melted chocolate into the cases and tip to coat evenly. Pour off excess chocolate, leave to set, and apply a second coat if desired. Fill the cups with the appropriate centers.

INDEX

Apricot-Glaze White Orange Pudding, 137
Baked Alaska, 142
Banana Choc-Chip Cooking, 133
Black-Bottom Lemon tartlets, 92
Bow Ties, 159
Buche de Noel, 75
Butterfly Cakes, 64
Charlotte Louise, 114

Cherry Chocolate Crunch, 73
Chocolate Mint Cup Cakes. 66
Chocolate Curls, 12
Chocolate Leaves, 13
Chocolate Amarreti Cookies, 16
Chocolate and Peacan pie, 87
Chocolate and Strwberry Frozen Daquoise, 109
Chocolate Boxes, 55
Chocolate Butter Biscuits, 37
Chocolate Caramel Popcorn, 177
Chocolate Chiffon Pie, 95
Chocolate Chip Cake, 69
Choclate Chunk chocolate Drops, 15
Chocolate Crackle Tops, 24
Chocolate Crean Pie, 83
Chocolate Crepes, 139
Chocolate Crispies, 30
Chocolate Crunch Animals, 185
Chocolate Cut-Outs, 12
Chocolate Eggs, 155
Chocolate Frozen Yogurt, 104
Chocolate Meringues, 65
Chocolate Mousse, 105
Chocolate Pavlova, 103
Chocolate Pecan Torte, 57
Chocolate and Pinenut Tart, 132
Chocolate Pots de Créme, 126
Chocolate Roulade, 125
Chocolate Rum Cake, 71
Chocolate Souffle, 131
Chocolate Tiramisu, 99
Chocolate Trifle, 123
Chocolate Turtles, 151
Chocolate-Chestnut-Roulade, 77
Chocolate-Coated Raspberry Truffles, 182
Chocolate-Coated Toffee, 147
Chocolate-Dipped Caramel Apples, 163
Chocolate-Dipped Fruit, 171
Chocolate-Mint Crisps, 167
Chocolate-Mint Cake, 66
Chocolate-Mint Sandwich Cookies , 20
Chocolate-Stuffed Figs and Prunes, 175
Chunky Chocolate Brownies with Fudge Glaze, 43

Cinnamon Chocolate Pain Perdu, 135
Classic Brownies, 40
Classic Devil's Food Cake, 79
Cocoa Brownies with Milk Chocolate and Walnut Topping, 46
Coconut Bonfires, 184
Coconut Ice, 13
Cream-Cheese Marbled Brownies, 59
Dobos Torte, 36
Double Chocolate Peppermint, 118
Easter Egg, 169

Easy Chocolate Truffles, 161
Family Chocolate Cake, 53
Florentines, 29
Fruited White Chocolate Bavarian Cream, 113
Ginger Bells, 173

Highball Cups, 189
Honeycamb Chunks, 172
Icy Christmas Puddings, 149
Luxury Macaroons, 22
Magic Chocolate Dessert, 140
Meringue Mushrooms, 157
Milk Chocolate and Pistachio-Coated Truffles, 186
Mississippi Mud Pie, 85
Mushroom Cake, 48
Peanut Butter Cornets, 179
Pears and Chocolate Sauce, 115
Piped Designs, 12
Profiteroles, 107
Prune and Chocolate Pieces, 180
Raspberry Chocolate Eclairs, 60
Red Velvet Cake, 63
Rich Chocolate Ice Cream, 110
Rich Chocolate Meringue Pie, 91
Rich Mocha Refidgerator Cake, 100
Rocky Road Lollipops, 179
Sachertorte, 41
Saucy Chocolate Cakes, 39
St. Valentine's Casket, 165
Suprise Chocolate Ring, 45
Triple Chocolate Cheesecake, 51
Triple Chocolate Mousse Parfaits, 121
Triple Decker Squares, 23
Tropical Delights, 164
Truffles, 27
Viennese Chocolate Cookies, 19
White Chocolate and Coconut Layer Cake, 35
White Chocolate Fruite Fools in Chocolate Cups, 116
White Chocolate Fudge Layer, 153
White Chocolate Mousse and Strawberry Tart, 89